WHY AM I SICK?

WHY AM I SICK?

How to Find Out What's Really Wrong Using

ADVANCED CLEARING ENERGETICS™

RICHARD FLOOK

HAY HOUSE

Carlsbad, California • New York City
London • Sydney • New Delhi

Published in the United Kingdom by:
Hay House UK Ltd, The Sixth Floor, Watson House,
54 Baker Street, London W1U 7BU
Tel: +44 (0)20 3927 7290; Fax: +44 (0)20 3927 7291
www.hayhouse.co.uk

Published in the United States of America by:
Hay House Inc., PO Box 5100, Carlsbad, CA 92018-5100
Tel: (1) 760 431 7695 or (800) 654 5126
Fax: (1) 760 431 6948 or (800) 650 5115
www.hayhouse.com

Published in Australia by:
Hay House Australia Ltd, 18/36 Ralph St, Alexandria NSW 2015
Tel: (61) 2 9669 4299; Fax: (61) 2 9669 4144
www.hayhouse.com.au

Published in India by:
Hay House Publishers India, Muskaan Complex, Plot No.3, B-2,
Vasant Kunj, New Delhi 110 070
Tel: (91) 11 4176 1620; Fax: (91) 11 4176 1630
www.hayhouse.co.in

A catalogue record for this book is available from the British Library.

ISBN: 978-1-4019-4389-9

CONTENTS

ACKNOWLEDGMENTS

My mother left my father when I was six. She moved hundreds of miles away north of where I lived in Bristol, in the southwest region of the UK. By the time I was 12, she had died of cancer. It was this event that ultimately led to my writing this book. I hope that the death of my mother, Anne Richardson (Flook), has not been in vain. I wish that she could be here, reading this book. I'm proud that my father, Julian Flook, will see the fruits of my labors, as he has supported me in my pursuit of understanding.

Following my parents' divorce, I found my father's relationships difficult to accept; it took a long time for me to forgive him. However, now that I have a son of my own, I understand how challenging it is being a parent. We all make mistakes – after all, we are only human. He has had his fair share of illnesses and issues. His support has been inspiring, and without him you wouldn't be reading this book.

My incredible wife, Kristin Watson-Flook, has patiently observed and assisted me in this book. Little does she know how her stability and groundedness have made this book into a reality. When we decided to change our business from an NLP training company to what has become Advanced Clearing Energetics™, we both knew it would be challenging, and Kristin has stuck by me through thick and thin. My learning and regular free consultations, as I strived to fully understand how Advanced Clearing Energetics works for people in real life, meant our income dropped by two-thirds of what we earned from NLP. I am glad to say it has paid off; this information is so valuable for everyone and I now provide training worldwide.

And, of course, I want to thank my son, Oliver. Anyone who has children will understand why I want to acknowledge him, because our children are our greatest teachers.

FOREWORD

BY KARL DAWSON
AND SASHA ALLENBY

As an Emotional Freedom Techniques (EFT)[1] Master, I've been on the cutting edge of the personal-development industry for a number of years. As for many people, this particular journey started with my own health issues.

From 2001 to 2002, I'd become increasingly ill with chronic fatigue, multiple allergies, inflammation, and metabolism, and blood-sugar regulation issues. While recovering from these conditions, I was drawn to EFT and soon became a therapist, trainer, and eventually an EFT Master. In this time, I drew a disproportionate number of clients and trainees who were also overcoming serious illness and disease. The universe has a way of sending not only those who are on a similar path but also, if we pay attention, the solutions to our problems. So while I looked for the answers to help my clients and myself heal, I was lucky enough to find wonderful teachers from around the world. Gary Craig, the creator of EFT, was one such teacher. Donna Gates, the founder of the Body Ecology Diet, and cellular biologist Dr. Bruce Lipton, were other pioneering and inspiring teachers, whose incredible knowledge helped me to make sense of and understand the conditions that I and others were experiencing – health conditions for which the modern medical model had no solution.

Armed with a wealth of information from these great people, I developed EFT for Serious Disease Training, which has been popular with medical professionals, therapists, and laypeople alike. My training explains how eventually, as we age, our early traumas and childhood experiences, if left unresolved, often manifest as a myriad of diseases, as the body tries to adapt the subconscious mind's mistaken perceptions of self and the environment. As well as identifying the problem, my training helped to address the solution, showing how these conditions can be resolved with EFT.

On my journey, I was fortunate to meet and train with Richard Flook, and learn his invaluable system now named Advanced Clearing Energetics. Time and again I've been able to help clients, trainees, and workshop attendees locate the underlying emotional cause of disease with pinpoint accuracy, and resolve it with EFT. I've seen great results working with chronic fatigue syndrome, rheumatoid arthritis, multiple sclerosis (MS), irritable bowel syndrome (IBS), diabetes, asthma, cancer, Crohn's disease, colitis, vitiligo, alopecia, hypothyroidism, anxiety, panic attacks, stress, and depression, among many other physical and emotional conditions. These results have been greatly accelerated thanks to Advanced Clearing Energetics.

Several years ago I developed an advance in EFT, a technique called 'Matrix Reimprinting.' Combining EFT with quantum physics and the developments in the new sciences, Matrix Reimprinting is a powerful tool for personal transformation. Richard fondly refers to Matrix Reimprinting and Advanced Clearing Energetics as a match made in heaven! The reason being that you can work directly with parts of yourself that have split off due to previous life traumas with Matrix Reimprinting and identify which traumas have specifically caused which disease with Advanced Clearing Energetics. So with simple analysis you can quickly get to the root of any disease condition using Advanced Clearing Energetics and resolve it using Matrix Reimprinting.

In 2008, with our shared passion to unite these two techniques, Richard and I filmed a three-day training course, in which we combined our knowledge. Richard skillfully questioned workshop participants about their existing medical conditions, identifying the life trauma(s) that had triggered them, while I resolved the stress and energetic disruption around the memory and installed more supportive memories using Matrix Reimprinting.

The results of this training were phenomenal! We worked with one workshop attendee and resolved her bipolar affective disorder in 50 minutes. With the accuracy of Advanced Clearing Energetics, we identified the root cause of the condition – three early life traumas – and with Matrix Reimprinting we reprogrammed these traumas. Of course, we might have eventually resolved this condition with Matrix Reimprinting alone, but without Advanced Clearing Energetics it would have taken months of systematically working on different life traumas in the hope of stumbling across the ones that caused the condition. Also, some of the traumas experienced are not available to the person consciously, so the ones causing the disease may remain hidden. But with Advanced Clearing Energetics, conditions and issues can be found accurately and precisely, enabling outstanding results.

I am, therefore, very pleased that Richard has written this book. There is, of course, much more to Advanced Clearing Energetics than just resolving trauma, and *Why Am I Sick?* explains this very accurately. This book contains a wealth of resources for doctors, medical professionals, psychotherapists, holistic therapists, and nutritionists, as well as all those wanting to identify the root cause of their health conditions. It is the much-needed missing link between therapeutic practice and the science behind sickness and disease. It is my hope that this book finds itself on the shelf of every practitioner who is serious about helping his or her clients to recover. It will certainly be at the top of the recommended reading list on my Matrix Reimprinting training courses.

Karl Dawson, co-author of
Matrix Reimprinting Using EFT

Like Karl, my journey started with debilitating illness – an illness that left me bedridden for several years up until 2005. In those days, I still bought into the model of reality where I believed I was an unfortunate victim of chronic fatigue syndrome, and my initial perception was that it had happened to me because I was unlucky. In reality, the disease I experienced was the single biggest gift of my life, and initiated such a huge transformation that I will be eternally grateful for the experience. But it took some time for my perception to shift and see it that way, so if you're reading this book because you're experiencing long-term illness or are supporting someone who is, I appreciate that you may not share this view at this stage of your experience.

My turning point came on a day like any other, when I found myself lying in bed repeating my mantra of how awful my life was, and how my life was, to all intents and purposes, over. But, on this particular day, I heard myself and had the realization that, although I wasn't to blame for my suffering, I was certainly enhancing it with my thoughts and my behavior. In that moment, I took responsibility for my experience and subsequently my healing.

What became apparent was that taking responsibility for my actions was far easier than taking control of my thoughts. I tried a myriad of positive-thinking techniques, only to find that as soon as I took my 'eye' off my thoughts, they would return to the same mantras of self-defeat, common to my physical condition. That's when I discovered EFT (Emotional Freedom Techniques). Initially, I was drawn to the technique because I learned that it could help with physical pain. In fact, my first experience of EFT reduced the physical pain in my legs significantly within five minutes – a pain that had plagued me for several years. But much deeper than that was what I came to discover through EFT – the link between the myriad of life traumas I had experienced and my physical condition. By connecting with Karl Dawson and using these techniques to address unresolved trauma, I found that my body healed simultaneously.

When I first met Richard Flook, I was fascinated to learn how accurately these life traumas could be connected to a physical condition. In fact, Richard could pinpoint with startling accuracy the source of a physical disease and the specific trauma that needed to be addressed to initiate and instigate the return to wellness. This proved very useful for my own healing, as not only did I have chronic fatigue syndrome, but I had also been challenged with bipolar affective disorder (manic depression) for 20 years. Working with Karl and later with Richard, I overcame this condition completely, and I've since witnessed other seemingly 'miraculous' healings from countless conditions that have no recognized solution.

I am therefore delighted that Richard has written this book. It is my hope that the healing I experienced doesn't become confined to the realms of the miraculous, but instead becomes commonplace, as more and more people learn the link between their traumatic life experiences and their own disease process, and resolve them with Advanced Clearing Energetics. This book is a fine and comprehensive answer to a myriad of health challenges. It gives hope to those who have long since surrendered to their condition, and practical tools to resolve the challenges that prevent people from experiencing the health that is their birthright. It is my hope that every doctor, alternative therapist, psychiatrist – everyone that has a vested interest in the healing of others – reads this book and applies its principles. It has the potential to create a wellness revolution that we could only dream of, and I believe it will take pride of place among the books of the twenty-first century, which challenge the current paradigm and offer a new medical model of reality.

Sasha Allenby, co-author of
Matrix Reimprinting Using EFT

A NEW UNDERSTANDING

'There is no education like adversity.'

Benjamin Disraeli, British Prime Minister (1804–1881)

Why Am I Sick? is about how trapped energy in the body can show up as disease, psychological issues, or some other issue or complaint; and how a person can go about identifying that trapped energy by using Advanced Clearing Energetics.

This information goes completely against the present thinking of traditional medicine, although I've tried to be open and give my reasons why I believe the present system is flawed, with evidence to prove each point. However, the information is controversial and designed to make you think differently about disease, why we get it, and how to solve it using approaches that integrate traditional, alternative, energetic, and complementary therapies.

If you're suffering from a disease of any sort and reading this book to find a solution to your issue, I advise you to get a medical diagnosis first. If you already have a diagnosis and are thinking about certain therapies, whether traditional, complementary, energetic, or alternative, then this book will open your eyes as to why you have your disease and the symptoms you may be experiencing. You can then, if you choose, find an Advanced Clearing Energetics practitioner to work with you, alongside your medical practitioner, to find the right integrative solution for your issue. There is a growing database of licensed practitioners on www.advancedclearingenergetics.com.

If you're a practitioner, then it is equally important to get a medical diagnosis for your client before you work on any disease or issue. An Advanced Clearing Energetics practitioner can assist you by answering why your client has a particular issue; they can work with you to help solve your client's underlying problem, and this may also mean working alongside a medical practitioner.

So the purpose of this book is to describe some of the processes behind Advanced Clearing Energetics, which I believe explains how disease works. If you want to learn more about it, there are many programs available to download and a list of live training courses at www.advancedclearingenergetics.com

CHAPTER 1

THE BEGINNING OF ADVANCED CLEARING ENERGETICS

'The greatest mistake in the treatment of diseases is that there are physicians for the body and physicians for the soul, although the two cannot be separated.'

Plato, Greek philosopher and playwright

It was 10.30 a.m. on a cold winter's day in 1976. I was 12 years old and walking up a small hill to a classroom at the school I attended in Bath, southwest UK. Tears flowed down my cheeks uncontrollably. I couldn't stop them, but I sobbed silently. I didn't want my school friends to see me – boys don't cry. I walked alone. It was a horrible, horrible day. However, with hindsight, it was an important one. It was the day that I was to make one of the most fundamental decisions of my life, a decision that would shape me and take me on an incredible journey, which until that time I hadn't foreseen in any way, a decision the importance of which I wouldn't realize for another 28 years.

My father had woken me that morning as he did every day, but instead of popping his head around the door in his usual jovial manner, he walked silently into my room and I could feel that something was wrong, as he was so obviously different. He sat for a moment, looking at me and shaking his head slowly from side to side. I can still remember his saddened face. He looked away as he spoke, his words full of grief: 'I don't know how to tell you, you know your mum was very ill, and I'm so sorry, Richard, she died late last night.'

My parents had divorced six years earlier and my mother noticed lumps in her left breast a few years later. By that time she'd remarried and moved a ten-hour car journey away from where my father, my two brothers, and I lived. We saw her only occasionally, and it was an extremely traumatic time for my brothers and myself – we missed her terribly. Much later I understood that this separation and worry about her three boys would be the cause of her breast cancer, subsequent complications, and her death.

Wanting to find out *why* she died so tragically and so young started me on a journey that eventually led me to set up Advanced Clearing Energetics, and help thousands of people understand what to this day remains unknown to the medical profession – why we get sick.

The flaw in traditional medicine

Don't get me wrong; medical doctors do a great job of diagnosing symptoms, whether it's heart disease or eczema; and then treating the symptoms with an appropriate treatment. But they still can't tell us what 'causes' disease to occur.

Medical science (and many alternative and complementary practices) theorizes that disease is an error of the body, and therefore therapy involves suppressing, killing, or shrinking the issue: e.g., radiation, surgery, or drug therapies. The diagnosis is simple – the body has done something wrong; it is weak or out of balance, and as a result of this, the disease has attacked in that place.

We've been taught to believe that, apart from adopting healthy lifestyle habits, disease is beyond our control; it is not our fault and therefore the issue/problem has nothing to do with us. What we think has nothing to do with disease. The mind and body are not connected. And with this belief most people turn to their medical practitioners and ask them to make them well again: 'Cut it out, zap it, give me drugs to kill the germs, do whatever you want to do to me; just get rid of it and make me well again.'

This approach has worked for many years, and certainly traditional medical techniques have had a profound effect on the world's general health and longevity over the last 100 years or so. It has driven the pharmaceutical industry relentlessly to develop newer, better, and more dynamic interventions – some of them brilliant. Plus, that's what we want, isn't it? A magic pill to pop and then be cured; what could be simpler? And, until recently, there has been a lack of proof of the body–mind connection, so who can blame the doctors or the pharmaceutical industry or society for this behavior?

However, why doesn't this system of 'curing' people work *all* the time? Time and time again I come across people who are unhappy with the cripplingly expensive, chemical, pill-popping culture, as it usually only masks the symptoms; and the drugs often create more side effects than the original issue. It's also strange that in the last 20 years, medical practitioners are no longer at the top of the social ladder. Honored in the past for their magical abilities to cure every ailment, they are now more likely to be sued for malpractice than hailed as healers.

There is also the fact that we have an enormous pharmaceutical industry, which plays a massive part in society by keeping government health policy focused on only one system of healing – using chemical resolutions to treat disease, when clearly there is a wealth of evidence proving that this chemical approach accounts for only a small part of the disease jigsaw puzzle.

What's gone wrong?

I can only speculate on the answer to that question as the facts are still unavailable, but I have some thoughts on this matter, and when you've finished reading this book, I believe you may think the same way, too.

For example, are you aware that 60 years ago the medical intervention for cancer was chemotherapy, radiation, and surgery? But at the time it was still in its infancy and experimental. Today the same treatments, with the addition of a little hormone therapy, are still used with cancer patients; and survival rates, despite reported improvements and a huge amount of research worldwide, remain unchanged.

In *Questioning Chemotherapy*, Ralph Moss PhD talks about how chemotherapy improves cancer patients' survival by 30 percent. Sounds good, but what does that 30 percent mean? Do people live longer and without recurrence? How are these statistics compiled? Personal supervision? Or by carefully controlled clinical trials?

Ralph Moss explains that the 30 percent often quoted tells people how long they will live without signs of the disease, but doesn't tell them if they will actually live any longer if they hadn't had chemotherapy.

He illustrates this point by describing ten randomized controlled trials (RCTs are the gold standard of medical research) of chemotherapy for node-negative breast cancer, which did reduce the rate of recurrence by about one-third but had no visible effect on survival. (An example of the 30 percent improvement often quoted.)

This may surprise you, as the media frequently report dramatic improvements in cancer treatments. However, it seems that the truth isn't as good as we've been led to believe. Yes, breast-cancer recurrence rates are down by 50 percent over the past 30 years, which implies that survival rates are up by 50 percent due to new treatments. Sadly, this is not the case, as most of these efforts are down to better screening, smoking cessation, and education, not new and improved treatments.

When one considers the trillions of dollars, often donated by charities, spent on the so-called war against cancer (not to mention heart disease, diabetes, and other common diseases), these improvements don't add up. How many more people have to die before medical science starts to look elsewhere than in the bottom of a petri dish, to establish that disease is a sequence triggered by changes in environmental conditions in a 'live' human being and not something that a single isolated defective cell decides to do without cause, reason, or explanation? Even a person with a defective gene who suddenly develops a disease, after being healthy, must have had something happen to trigger that gene to change it.

Same disease, different philosophy

You probably think that the basic treatment and philosophies for most diseases are the same worldwide. However, every country has a different approach to treating disease. For example, did you know that there are four separate philosophies for the cause of diabetes and therefore the focus of research and treatment? Let's look at them:

⦿ In the UK it is believed that diabetes is hereditary and genetic, hence a lot of money is being put into stem-cell research.

⦿ In other parts of the West, it is believed that diabetes is due to a virus.

⦿ In Israel, scientists are researching how the beta islet cells (in the pancreas, and which produce insulin) communicate with each other; they have found that these cells build tubes that talk to each other, and theorize that in diabetics these cells are too busy chatting among themselves to do what the body wants them to do.

⦿ In the East, there is a theory that diabetes may be due to trace elements being out of balance in the body; if there is too much of one specific element, the insulin molecules clump together in sixes and are ineffective.

These are four completely different explanations as to the cause of diabetes, and the same is true in practically all diseases. Undoubtedly all of them could be right. However, the money goes into researching what is in vogue at the time in that particular country. What this means for the patient is that medical research is a lotto based on who has the cash, the research team that thinks they might be able to prove something is happening, and what drugs can be developed from this research. The sales of the drug pay for the investment in research, and what is left over is profit for the company. Let's be clear, I don't think anyone is conspiring to do anything wrong here, but the process of the development of a wonder cure is not as idealistic as we may think.

Over the last 100 years, we've put a man on the moon, built wonderful new buildings and other engineering masterpieces, and have done things with technology that were pure science fiction in the 1950s; just look at an iPad or smartphone and you can see how technology is changing everything in our world. Meanwhile, quantum physics tells us we are not who we think we are, and that matter is just pure energy, while quantum mechanics has been able to explain some of the world's most incredible phenomena. We can blow up the world 1,000 times over with nuclear weapons, see things at a million times magnification through electron microscopes, and through genetics we can determine many of the imprints that make up the biological blueprint of our bodies.

Despite all these advances, the medical profession remains unquestioning about the cause of disease and seems content with the 'not known' conclusion.

State of health

Cancer affects six to seven million people worldwide and is on the increase, according to the World Health Organization (WHO).[1] It is the third biggest killer after heart disease and death due to medical intervention. Yes, you did read it correctly. Medical intervention that goes wrong is either the first or second biggest killer. The figures are rarely mentioned and seem to be a closely guarded secret, but they are there.[2]

However, needless to say, without medical care many unnecessary deaths would also occur. It's a catch-22. If modern medicine is introduced into a developing country, the survival rate increases dramatically. People's lives get better; they don't die of cholera, malaria, or other diseases such as smallpox. Cheap cataract operations, and modern surgical techniques applied in these countries, improve and save many more lives. Drugs have solved and do solve many problems, and some of the interventions are truly amazing and are definitely lifesavers.

The question I want to address, however, is that of stress and disease. There is a huge amount of research indicating that there is a link between chronic stress and most of the major diseases,[3] but it is usually considered a discrete issue of the mind rather than a cause of more serious diseases and issues in the body.

So why, if stress is implicated as a factor in disease, do medical professionals continue to prescribe drugs that only mask the symptoms, rather than addressing the issue of stress itself?

SKIN ISSUES – SEPARATION ANXIETY

On a flight to Australia I happened to be sitting next to Jessica, who asked my advice about a skin problem, which had appeared all over her neck and chest/belly area in the last four weeks. Skin problems such as this are often due to separation issues, and she told me that her fiancé had decided to go to Australia to set up a business. As she spoke, she went red and her eyes became watery, so I asked her, 'Why don't you pack in your job and move over to Australia with him?' She went bright red again and tears welled up in her eyes. Clearly she was under a lot of stress. She told me that she could cope with him being away but couldn't bear being away from her family.

Her doctor had no idea what caused the skin problem or why it started. But it was obvious when I pointed it out to her. The skin issue prevented her from feeling the separation (you literally don't feel the separation on your skin because it goes numb; this is what I call the 'Stress Stage' of the disease, which I'll discuss in more detail in Chapter 5 (see page 91). However, rather than seeing that her issue was due to the stress of separation, her doctor prescribed a steroid cream, which has the long-term effects of thinning the skin and, most likely, exacerbating the condition.

This is just the first of many case studies that you'll read about in this book, but Jessica's story goes some way to explaining why medical doctors have such a difficult time diagnosing an issue; it is due to the fact that they are guessing all the time as to what is causing the problem. Faced with a medical issue, their only options are drug therapies or surgery. There is often no link made between the mind and the body to reveal why a disease is there and what might be the next set of symptoms. The drugs they prescribe have one side effect followed by another, the explanation of which is based on old science, but this is not how the body behaves.

Those doctors who are dissatisfied with simply being drug pushers have to reinvent themselves and pursue a career in a different way. Three people who come to mind who have successfully achieved this are Dr. Deepak Chopra, author of *Quantum Healing*; Dr. Christiane Northrup, who has written many books including *Women's Bodies, Women's Wisdom*; and Dr. Carl Simonton, one of the forefathers in this modern approach where the mind and body are totally linked. He wrote an amazing book called *Getting Well Again*.

Doctors, stuck in their traditional practices, are not encouraged to look at other possible causes of a problem. This means that even in a modern hospital, the consultant deals only with his or her specialty, with little regard for other specialists. Psychologists rarely mix with medical doctors, as the mind has no perceived connection with disease even in the one place it should – your hospital.

So why is this *not* happening?

Medicine means business

We all assume that every doctor is as good as the next, but we never think that of a business owner or designer. Each doctor has a different character and, since conventional medicine is based on hypothesis with no real science to back up why something works or not, doctors can be easily led. This is where business does come into the equation – in the form of drug companies.

Call me cynical, but the fact remains that money, not cures, is the driving force in the pharmaceutical industry. And if I were in the pharmaceutical industry, I would be rubbing my hands together because I'd know my job would have been done; billions of dollars of taxpayers' and medical insurance money going right into my pockets. Medicine is driven by money, and if you know how to play the game, you can win the jackpot regularly.

This issue with the pharmaceutical industry, the medical profession, and the political situation is unlikely to change. The only thing that will affect change will be public awareness. I believe that if people start asking the really challenging questions when diagnosed with a disease, then the medical profession will be forced to review their outdated hypotheses about disease. People haven't started asking these questions yet. But they will, and when they do, the Berlin Wall of the medical profession will come tumbling down. I predict that the doctors who have been keeping this status quo will be left standing with nothing on except their white coats, saying 'Oops! We made a mistake.' The information in this book is too challenging for them to admit they have made a mistake, but ultimately, they will. In the meantime, start thinking about the questions that your medical practitioner can't answer, simple questions such as:

- What caused my disease? Why don't you know?
- You're saying my body has made a mistake, but why has it done this to me?
- Why do you always have to remove the affected part? Have you ever thought it might be there for a reason?
- What makes you so sure that my stressful life hasn't caused this disease, and why can't you prove it?
- How do you know I will die if I don't have this treatment, and on what basis can you say that?

- What is the life expectancy for people who don't take this drug?
- Why do these drugs' side effects seem worse than the disease the drugs are supposed to be curing?
- Over the last 50 years, how successful has this type of drug regime been?
- How do you know that the mind is not directly connected to the body? Prove it!
- Why don't you have connected thinking in the medical profession?

Change will happen, but not because the medical profession realizes that the body has made a mistake or that the mind and body are interlinked. The change will happen through political and economic forces and due to millions of people asking the questions, only to be given answers that consistently don't add up.

The mind–body connection

If it sounds as if I'm criticizing the medical profession. I'm not. Doctors do incredible work and save millions of lives, but I do challenge their outdated belief system. What I believe, and found to be true in my work with Advanced Clearing Energetics, is that there is a factor that runs through all diseases; there is a specific 'cause,' which is based on the latest research and understanding about disease.

We know that disease is the result of a trigger; we know that, and wonderful things *are* happening in science, as it evolves and challenges our current paradigms of thinking. But when it comes to medicine, these changes have gone unacknowledged or even unconsidered. Take, for example, the implications of epigenetics, the new science born out of genetic research, which is challenging the very philosophies of modern medicine regarding how diseases are created.

Professor Wolf Reik at the Babraham Institute in Cambridge, UK, has spent years studying this hidden ghost world of DNA and epigenetics. He has found that merely manipulating the embryos of mice, without changing their DNA in any way, is enough to trigger 'switches' that turn a gene's expression on or off.[4] His work[5] has shown that these switches can be inherited, which means that a shocking 'memory' of an event could be passed down through generations. In other words, a simple environmental effect can switch a gene's expression on or off, and this change can be inherited.

For example, a great-grandparent who went through a famine passes on an expression of a gene that tells the body to gorge when it can, and store excess food so it won't starve to death in the future. Parents who limit a grandchild's intake of food, for health reasons, could be causing the child's body to trigger this inherited gene's expression and the child to become clinically obese.

This means that a shocking experience suffered by a great-grandparent is remembered and passed down intelligently through the gene pool to a grandchild. If that grandchild experiences something environmentally similar to that experienced by the great-grandparent, that event then triggers the same learned pattern; it causes that key specific gene, with the memory stored in it, to alter its expression (not create a new gene or change its coding, but to switch on how that gene expresses itself in the body).

This goes a long way to prove that genes and the environment are not mutually exclusive, but inextricably intertwined; the environment affects the gene. The environment is linked to why we get sick.

The research into epigenetics is also backed up by discoveries showing that it is the cell membrane and not the DNA that is responsible for determining how the DNA switches itself on and off. Cells change their structure and function based on their environment.[6]

Our thoughts also affect our body. It has now been proven through neuropeptide research that the mind and body are connected as one. This means that as you think, you affect the whole of your neurology, and this forms the basis of applied kinesiology (which uses muscle testing to find the cause of disease and can be used in Advanced Clearing Energetics). We now know so much more about the body and what it is doing than we did in the 1950s, when medicine promised us a pill or drug that could cure everything.

So why hasn't the medical fraternity learned from these breakthroughs? It's as if these doctors are burying their heads in the sand and ignoring what has happened around them in the last 50 to 60 years. A simple example of this is if you give someone a drug that is supposed to solve a complex issue, which has been tested using Newtonian physics, developed by Sir Isaac Newton (1643–1727), but we now know the body works in a quantum mechanical way, as discovered in the 1920s.

A drug affects every part of the body, not just the organ it is designed to treat. Consequently, you get side effects. In this instance, the medical fraternity is using science based on a system that is more than 350 years old (Newtonian physics). The literature explaining quantum biology is available, but it seems as if the medical fraternity refuses to listen. Bruce Lipton's book *The Biology of Belief* covers this whole premise of quantum science applied to medicine very well.

There are many more examples of this ostrich head-burying phenomenon, some of which I will mention later, but one of the craziest is that the cause of practically every illness, disease, pain, or disorder is not known. It is true, your doctor and all the medical scientists out in the world don't know what causes 99 percent or most of the diseases. Look in any medical dictionary or on the internet and you'll find 'the cause of this disease is not known.' There are hypotheses as to what may cause a disease, but they remain categorically unproven.

What seems to be happening in medicine is all based on old science and a lot of guesswork as to what is going on inside people when they have a disease. The science is there and has been for many years, but the medical industry refuses to accept or implement any of this new science. Meanwhile, the $50 billion-a-year cancer treatment business[7] is increasing by 15 percent every year[8] and, according to an article in the *New York Times* written by Andrew Pollack in September 2009:

> *'Virtually every large pharmaceutical company seems to have discovered cancer, and a substantial portion of the smaller biotechnology companies are focused on it as well. Together, the companies are pouring billions of dollars into developing cancer drugs.'*

It seems the medical fraternity isn't really interested in the cause of a disease: why a lump appears in a breast, why someone gets eczema, why a person suffers horrendously with IBS, why a cyst appears, why a person gets chronic backaches. What causes any of these issues cannot be explained, so the cause is ignored, as is the patient who asks why their disease is there, and why at this moment in his or her life? The doctor can't tell these patients because they simply don't know.

It poses a real question that no one has asked the medical fraternity: 'How can you claim to cure a disease (and medical practitioners are the only people who can claim to cure someone) if you don't know what caused it to occur in the first place?'

Please understand me, I believe the medical fraternity and doctors do a magnificent job; they are fantastic diagnosticians. When it comes to breaking a limb or an emergency situation, for example, the ER is the place to go. Plastic surgery is incredible, and many drugs are lifesavers. It is just the flawed way of approaching the cause of disease that I believe must change.

As a youngster, I would listen with bated breath as the next cure for cancer was announced. Many decades on, I am still waiting. In fact, I've given up. Finding a pill, drug, serum, or treatment is unlikely to happen. We have thrown all the money we can at cancer, but where's the cure? When are all the people who dig their hands in their pockets to support the various cancer charities going to realize that no magic drug will ever be developed to 'cure' this disease? This way of looking at the body has not worked so far, and I'm prepared to say that this approach will not bring results in the future.

As I mentioned earlier, over the last 50 years many therapeutic interventions have remained the same. Those cancer-research scientists are still looking inside the body for the wonder drug instead of looking outside at the bigger picture, and at what has been going on in their own backyard. The attitude of the medical profession has not changed: the mind–body link has not been acknowledged; DNA is still regarded as the culprit for all diseases; and the medical profession has ignored many of the biological breakthroughs since the 1980s, some of which prove that it is the cell membrane that controls how DNA expresses itself. This means that the environment, everything that is going on outside the cell, has a massive impact on how the cell reacts inside.

DNA is dumb. It can be compared to the hard drive of a computer; it does nothing until it is told what to do. That message comes from the CPU (central processing unit – the main processing chip of a computer), which controls how the files are accessed and used. Why in modern medicine does consciousness, which is like the CPU, still play no part in telling the body what to do and what not to do, regardless of the undeniable evidence that proves that our thoughts affect our body? When it comes to so-called modern medicine, unfortunately I believe we are living in a bygone age. Advanced Clearing Energetics challenges that outdated perspective and is able to offer the answers.

How Advanced Clearing Energetics treats disease

Advanced Clearing Energetics uses a doctor's diagnosis and works backward from it to find the *original cause* of the disease, condition, or issue – the event that triggered the disease.

The trigger is usually a dramatic change in the environment – an event that is full of a lot of energy and which the body has no strategy for dealing with. It's something so stressful that it causes the DNA to change and create disease. Events such as being ripped away from someone we love, or a sudden change of behavior as with addictions, for example. The feelings shock the body because they are so unfamiliar and the person doesn't know how to deal with them.

Medical practitioners treat the symptom with the aim of getting rid of the disease by using drugs, surgery, heating, freezing, or other therapies to make the symptoms disappear. In Advanced Clearing Energetics, treatment means helping the person learn from and clear the trapped energy of the stressful event that produced the disease, pain, or psychological issue; the body then repairs itself, something it does naturally.

We'll be looking at the evidence in more detail in Chapter 3, but for now let's say that disease is due to stress, which we can say with certainty was passed down to us through past events, often before our birth and very commonly from our parents. Most people completely agree with this and say, 'I always knew stress caused disease,' and it was this understanding together with an unusual set of circumstances that caused me to set up Advanced Clearing Energetics.

The beginnings of Advanced Clearing Energetics

In 1992, while studying NLP (neuro-linguistic programming), I came across the brilliant work of Dr. Tad James, called Time-Line Therapy®. He said that the cause of cancer was a decision we make 12 to 36 months prior to the cancer showing up in the body. He mentioned some literature from a maverick German doctor, Dr. Geerd Hamer, and it was looking through this information that made me realize that there seemed to be an energetic component to disease – that a shock shows up in the brain and in an organ of a person, based on embryology (see p.167). Here was part of my answer to my mother's death, and it was the first thing that I had heard, in more than 20 years of searching for the cause of my mother's death, that actually made sense.

I continued researching this element of disease by training to become a master trainer in META-Medicine®, a diagnostic tool based on Hamer's work, which assists a trained practitioner in understanding the emotional event that causes a disease to occur. It was created to share Hamer's information with a wider international audience.

I was around at the start of META-Medicine, and over the following years I developed the material extensively. In the beginning it was all theory and, to be honest, didn't work very well, as it was very complicated and required medical training to understand how to make it work. However, by applying my extensive NLP knowledge, I changed META-Medicine considerably so practitioners could easily find the stressful event and apply their therapeutic intervention.

During this time, I also learned how to interpret the trapped energetic imprints that can be read in brain CT scans (computerized tomography, also known as CAT scans). From a brain CT scan, someone trained in this field can read the information and tell the subject their complete disease history.

I also worked with Karl Dawson, who introduced me to Matrix Reimprinting, and we had amazing success with one lady called Cathy when we cleared her bipolar disorder in 50 minutes (you can watch this by visiting www.whyamisick.com). And I was spurred on in my work by the amazing Karin Davidson, creator of Soul Reconnecting (www.howtotap.com); and Peter Fraser of NES Health who made some groundbreaking discoveries about how the mind and body hold trapped energy in its system. NES Health uses an advanced combination of acupuncture and homeopathy to measure the human body field, giving an energetic understanding of what is happening in the body (www.neshealth.com).

Over the next few years I developed my theories into the Meta Healing Process. I delivered training courses worldwide and on the internet. My students started to see similar results, and I knew I was on to something very special.

PERI-MENOPAUSE – AN EARLY SUCCESS STORY, FERTILITY ISSUES

One of my students consulted me because she had stopped menstruating. She was 44 and wanted to know why it had started so early. Menopause can happen earlier than normal due to a shock, so I asked her if she'd lost a child. She hadn't, but told me that she'd always wanted children, but her husband had made it clear that he didn't want them.

From my knowledge of reading CT scans, I knew that energy becomes trapped in the brain and the body in specific locations in line with embryology (see also pages 161–167). And from my knowledge of NLP, I also knew that this energy corresponded to a shock, meaning it had to have a visual element, auditory sound, a feeling, a taste, or smell to it. I also knew from being a trainer in hypnotherapy that you could talk to any organ in the body. So I asked my student to talk to her ovaries. What happened next was amazing. They spoke back.

Her ovaries were angry with her because she always put work before family. I then asked her to go to the brain location that represented her ovaries. Again, more information started to flow about how lost she felt in not having children. Then I asked her to go to the heart, and the shock that started the whole issue came up. It was an event that happened when she was looking at a new apartment with her husband. She mentioned something about the apartment not being big enough if they were ever to have children. It was her husband's reaction that completely shocked her. He became extremely angry and dismissed her, saying she would make a useless mother.

We worked on the shock and cleared out all the energy around these events and left it at that. I met her three months later, and she was delighted to tell me that her periods had returned. Many other changes had occurred as well. She spoke to her husband about the event that shocked her. Thankfully, he was amazingly supportive and they started to try for children, but also talked about adopting a child. She told me everything changed in a really amazing way that day.

In June 2011, I traveled again to see Peter Fraser in Spain. Over the previous few years I'd been integral in developing techniques that accelerated finding the shocks using NES brain infoceuticals: special bottles of water imprinted with specific energy, which communicate with the different embryonic layers; and a separate infoceutical called Liberator, which can be used to release trapped energy.

Peter had been working to integrate his energetic principles of the human body field into the Global Scaling work of Hartmut Müller. Global Scaling mathematically explains the scale and vibration of everything, such as how atoms come together to form compounds, and why our organs are the perfect size for our bodies, right up to why planets are the size they are. Together we were able to finally piece together what was really happening inside the body as a disease happened. It was not how either of us originally thought; in fact, it was far more beautiful than that. Neither of us really understood fully what we had discovered that day, but we both knew it was profound, because it was mathematical in nature; and meant we could piece together why, how, and what the body would do next in a disease.

While in Australia in August 2012, along with Rose Hayman and Cyril Bourke of the ZapHouse, I understood what Peter and I had put together. It is still incredible work, and I will share more of that in my next book, *How Can I Heal?*

The final piece of the puzzle came from Charles Matthew, who trained with Dr. Tad James, and showed me some very interesting techniques for clearing energy at a deep level. I deciphered his techniques and integrated them into all my previous work, combining them into one simple yet profound teaching – Advanced Clearing Energetics, which literally transforms pain into learning.

How Advanced Clearing Energetics works

In my research with Peter Fraser of NES Health, we established that during the original shocking event, the heart communicates with the brain and the guts, which in turn decide on the organ best suited to deal with the event. Which organ is picked is based on embryology (how we develop from an egg into a fetus; see pages 167–169) – basically how we are made. The organ then goes to work, altering itself as part of the whole process. Some simple examples of this would be:

◉ The guts dealing with something you can't digest causing, for example, IBS or food intolerance.

◉ The skin dealing with physical separation causing, for example, eczema.

◉ The muscles or limbs unable to support you through a problem causing, for example, back or joint pain.

◉ The brain going out of balance due to repeated sexual abuse at an early age causing, for example, drug or alcohol addictions.

After this an amazing chain of events occurs; the chosen organ changes itself to support the person through the situation, perhaps by growing or shrinking, adding or taking away cells, depending on the job with which it has been tasked. It is during these different stages that we experience symptoms, the very same symptoms that a medical practitioner labels 'disease.'

In Advanced Clearing Energetics we use this model of the heart, brain, organs, and guts, and then go back to the original imprint of the problem and clear the reason that caused the energy to become trapped. The result? The body returns to normality and health, repairing itself naturally. Digestive health returns, the skin heals, the muscles rebuild, and the urge to drink or take drugs stops.

The beginnings of an answer...

Advanced Clearing Energetics is not a cure; I've never cured anyone of a disease. Advanced Clearing Energetics is about transforming pain created by specific stressful events that cause certain diseases, into learning. By working back from symptoms labeled disease, psychological issues, or pain and through simple questioning, it is possible to release the underlying imprint that caused the epigenetic switches to be changed in our bodies, therefore allowing the body to complete its own healing and return to wellness.

It is important for me to say that Advanced Clearing Energetics doesn't supersede a conventional medical diagnosis. We also consider complementary, alternative, or energetic viewpoints; all of these disciplines have merit at some level. Advanced Clearing Energetics can work before, during, and after any therapeutic intervention except in the case of emergency life-threatening issues (which require immediate medical attention), and much rehabilitation work is as a result of accidents. However, in this instance, knowledge of Advanced Clearing Energetics can assist any medical practitioner in how to plan an intervention.

Advanced Clearing Energetics can also identify what caused the disease in the first place. It can explain the reasons why the body is showing symptoms (e.g., the size of a tumor), the length of a disease, why a disease becomes chronic. Also, important questions such as why a disease appears hereditary, what the next symptoms will be, where the person is within the disease process, how long a disease will take to complete its cycle, what will be the next stage and, therefore, what symptoms to expect.

Allergies, chronic or recurring diseases, water retention, epileptic seizures, migraines, and cardiac arrests can be explained. Plus, why we change our personality, our spiritual nature, our reaction to certain stimuli in the environment, and why we change socially.

With many new techniques that have come from Advanced Clearing Energetics, we are also seeing clients healing themselves with very few of the painful symptoms often associated with returning to wellness. We are also seeing magical changes in people's personalities, such as clinical depression lifting within hours, sprained or physically damaged ankles healing within a day, and swelling reducing right in front of a client's eyes. All of these seemingly miraculous changes can be explained scientifically as well.

In addition, metastasis (the development of secondary cancers) can finally be correctly explained, as can the role of microbes, bacteria, viruses, and fungi and why they are not the evil, nasty villains of nature that should be eliminated at all costs in order for a person to survive (see also page 184). Additionally, psychological issues such as depression, bulimia, bipolar disorder, acute anxiety, and other forms of neurosis and psychosis also have an answer and energetic solutions.

Advanced Clearing Energetics is really a way of clearing the energetic imprint that caused a disease to occur in the first place, and therefore allows the body to complete its healing naturally. It literally transforms pain into learning because it recognizes that the body creates a disease due to trapped energy in the mind, body, guts, and heart. Once you release the trapped energy by finding the reason for it and learning from that, then the body goes back into a natural flow. The disease corrects itself.

I meet many people who just want an answer to the question of their own disease. They want to know, 'Why am I sick?' and in my quest to understand my mother's death, I can now say that I know what caused her breast cancer. I know what caused it to spread to her lymph glands, her liver, and her bones. I know why she died and why chemotherapy, radiation, and surgery didn't work.

BREAST CANCER – MY MOTHER'S DEATH, AN INABILITY TO NURTURE

My mother developed cancer three years after leaving her sons; the emotional wrench she experienced when she realized her boys wouldn't be living with her was too much for her. She rationalized her decision; she chose love over her children. But being unable to nurture, and being separated from my brothers and me, are what caused the breast cancer to occur.

Women's breasts are the point of nurture, and after the worry of separation from the three boys began to subside, the left breast developed a tumor called a 'ductal carcinoma in situ' (a type of breast cancer that can develop as the milk ducts begin to repair). She battled with further shocks due to medical diagnosis and a mastectomy, which meant she no longer felt like a woman. Complications brought on by the surgery, radiation, and chemotherapy depleted her very life-source energy (the mitochondria).

My mother left my father to be with another man, who couldn't afford to feed and house her three boys; and she was only able to see us occasionally because she lived an eight- to ten-hour drive away. Understanding that her breast cancer was caused by the separation from her children, and that she could have prevented it, was a huge revelation to me; and has given me a massive mental release and closure on her tragic death.

In the next chapter, we'll explore why diseases happen. Is it because we caught a virus, our DNA is defective, or because we ate something that was contaminated through bacteria, or could it be more obvious than that? Or could it be due to something we all know about, but the medical profession and even complementary and alternative practitioners choose to ignore?

CHAPTER 2

ARE DISEASES, PAIN, OR CANCER A MISTAKE; OR DO THEY OCCUR FOR A REASON?

'When you treat a disease, first treat the mind.'

Taoist teaching

Time and again my clients tell me the same thing: 'Everything was finally going well, life was good, and then I got this problem, cancer, or debilitating pain. I'd been under a lot of pressure before then, and just as things were getting back to normal, wham, I got sick.'

Perhaps you've experienced this, too? After a long spell of hard work and stress, you're finally able to relax – maybe sitting by a pool or on the beach in an exotic location, with the chance to really enjoy yourself, and then you come down with the flu or gastroenteritis within days of arriving at the resort. Why?

Why does the body make a disease happen? Is it because the body has done something evil? Has God suddenly struck us down from afar because we swore under our breath at our parents when we were 17 and now, aged 35, we have to pay the price? Is it because our genetics are at fault, or are we such highly developed beings that we are more susceptible to disease? Does our body give out on us because our life is so stressful that it creates a disease to punish us because it can't cope?

Or is there another reason? Consider for a moment, could it perhaps be simply that the body is repairing itself after all the stress we have been through?

While you ponder that question, the following story illustrates why I realized that 'stress' is the ultimate cause of disease.

HERNIATED DISC – LACK OF SELF-ESTEEM

On the second day of running a two-day NLP business course in North Wales with Kristin (my business partner and soon to be my wife), the training was going well when I got out of my seat, ripped a page off a flip chart, and placed it on the wall behind us. This meant that I had to lean over to the left a little bit, not an unusual maneuver, but one that was a little tricky.
Then IT happened. A small pain crept across my lower back, focused on the left-hand side. The pain hurt and worried me, so I quickly sat back down, but the pain became even worse.

Somehow, and with help from Kristin, I managed to get through the rest of the training course, but all the time and for 18 months afterward, I asked: 'Why am I sick?' Why, when everything was going so well, did my back go? At the time, I hoped it was only a pulled muscle, but was worried because it felt like the same pain I'd experienced when I had a rugby accident at the age of 18. That pain had lasted ten years and I'd gotten rid of it during an NLP training course at the age of 28.

So why did I have this problem? Was there a reason for my back pain? Why was it there? Why did it happen to me at that exact time? I remember thinking about this at length because I knew, through NLP (Advanced Clearing Energetics was still in my future), that the mind was connected to the body. I asked this question over and over again. Why me and why then? What was the purpose for such a debilitating issue to happen to me at that specific time, especially since everything was going so well?

My doctor misdiagnosed my back pain as hereditary ankylosing spondylitis and suggested invasive treatments and pharmaceutical drugs, which, fortunately, I refused. And so over the next 18 months I continued to ask: 'Why am I in pain?' But despite consulting some of the top orthopedic surgeons, chiropractors, and other alternative and complementary specialists, they couldn't tell me what had caused my back problem. However, by that time I no longer cared. All I wanted was for the pain to disappear and to be able to walk again.

Finally, I had a brain CT scan read by a doctor trained to identify specific traumas in certain areas of the brain and their corresponding embryonic organ in the body (something I later trained to do). The trauma was identified as an event that had happened a couple of years earlier, which had severely affected my self-esteem. Therefore, my back pain was a result of feeling unable to stand up for myself and what I believed to be important.

Hearing this energetic diagnosis, everything fell into place. Prior to setting up the training company with Kristin, I'd experienced a shock from my then business partner, when he'd severely undermined my self-esteem while we were giving an NLP training course; it's what I did, it was my life. As a consequence, I decided not to go into partnership with him, and set up a new business. But the stress and sleeplessness due to the shock over many months meant a disc in my lower back degenerated and later herniated. During this time, I needed to be more flexible to cope with the stress, and the disc in my lower back was literally helping me find a different way to support myself through this problem and stopping me from allowing people to walk all over me.

Once I resolved the issue and set up my own business, then the disc herniated. It was excruciatingly painful, rendering me unable to walk more than 30ft without crying in pain. This pain was not the start of the disease; it was a later stage of a very precise healing process that the body goes through, which I'll discuss in a subsequent chapter.

However, this issue with my back also taught me more about myself. Since that time, my attitude about life has dramatically changed for the better, and I'm doing what I'm destined to do. My back problems almost made me lose everything I had worked for in my life. However, now I have no pain; I jog, run, walk, and *live a completely normal life. I've had an MRI scan, and it shows that the cartilage is no longer pressing against the nerves.*

As discussed in the previous chapter, medical science doesn't know the 'cause' of many of the most common diseases, believing that the body has just gone wrong. But what if medical science is mistaken and their 'error' theory is actually costing more lives than it saves?

Let us explore the medical arguments for thinking this way by starting with genes.

Do genes cause disease? Are all diseases inherited?

Gene research hasn't given us all the answers we thought it would. As an example, a gene was found that caused breast cancer. The laboratory that found it was naturally ecstatic and patented the genes BRCA1 and BRCA2 (BReast CAncer types 1 and 2), so they could develop therapies to 'cure' breast cancer. However, only 5 percent of women with breast cancer have these defective genes or one of the 200 mutations.[1] Unfortunately, like many of these promises, gene research doesn't seem to be able to offer the answer.[2]

The truth seems to be that the environment controls how a gene expresses itself. According to research carried out by Bruce Lipton, a popular cellular biologist and author, experiments on human cells have shown that if you provide a healthy environment for cells to grow, they multiply happily. Provide a less than optimal environment and they stop multiplying and show signs of sickness: 'cells

I was studying change their structure and function based on their environment.'[3]

In the past this wasn't apparent because most cell biologists didn't take into account the tissue cultures in which they grew their cells – their environment.[4] The effect that the environment has on our lives and therefore our cells has seemingly been ignored since DNA's genetic code was discovered in 1959. And even Charles Darwin regretted omitting the environment and the direct effect that food, climate, social interactions, and place have on individuals, independent of natural selection. In a letter to Moritz Wagner,[5] a German explorer and natural historian, Darwin wrote:

'In my Opinion, the greatest error which I have committed has been not allowing sufficient weight to the direct action of the environments, i.e., food, climate, etc., independently of natural selection.'

So can we say that the environment causes disease? Well yes, the theories all point toward this being true and there seems to be a wealth of evidence to prove this theory.[6-21] However, still more research needs to be done to confirm this fact for certain. Yet if this fact has been all but proven, why do the conventional medical professions (your medical practitioner), your well-trained complementary practitioner, or alternative practitioner still believe that the body has made an error? Genetics cannot all be wrong; it is very confusing.

We know that there *are* a few diseases that occur due to genetics: cystic fibrosis, Huntington's chorea, and beta thalassemia can all be blamed on genetic disorders, but single genetic disorders affect less than 2 percent of the population. Why is it that someone who is completely healthy suddenly develops one of these diseases later on in life, while others who have the defective gene never develop the disease?

And here's another puzzling thought: diseases such as heart disease, cancer, and diabetes are said to be the result of complex interactions of multiple genes and environmental factors. That is the latest thought behind these biggest killers in our Western civilization. Consider this strange fact – only 5 percent of cardiovascular and cancer patients can attribute their disease to heredity.[22] Therefore, as far as hereditary diseases are concerned, the evidence doesn't look good for the 'the body has made an error' fraternity.

Scientists have seldom found that one gene causes a trait or a disease. So what switches on these genes? Do genes control the body? Or is this a hypothesis, not a truth, as was pointed out in a paper called 'Metaphor and the roles of genes and development'?[23]

The environmental factor

The fact is that there are *no* scientific facts to prove that genes control the body. So if it is not the genes, could environment be the cause? We have to ask the question: could cells change, as the environment changes? Could gene expression switch on and off based on environmental conditions? Even though science has successfully proven that the body has not made a mistake, practically all medical research done today still focuses on the premise that the body is doing, or has done, something wrong. As an example, most cancer research is still trying to find the defective element or gene in the body, or studying the effects of killing a cancer cell using chemotherapy.[24]

'Defective' genes have nothing to do with the rapid growth of breast or any other cancer. In breast cancer, 'bad' genes are described as disrupted growth factor functions, yet no research has identified the source of the dysfunction. The normal way to designate genes is by a chromosome 'number' and 'arm.'[25] So-called defective breast cancer genes don't have these proper designations and are just theoretical. No cancer gene has ever been located and identified according to the combination of genetic bases and amino acid fault.[26]

I've noticed that all the studies into disease start off with the illness and work back to 'how can we make the body well again?' But what if the body already knows what to do? I personally think it does, as does Dr. L. Hashemzadeh-Boneh, a scientist who trained with me. The fact is that scientists are often 20 or so years ahead of medicine. Scientists know that the body responds to the environment, but the medical researchers don't listen to scientists.

This can be explained by looking at one of the most exciting areas of genetic research called 'epigenetics' (see page 122), the study of how a gene expression is switched on or off due to precise changes in our environment. Bruce Lipton, in *The Biology of Belief*, discusses how research has shown that the malignancy in a significant number of cancer patients is derived from environmentally induced epigenetic alterations and not defective genes.[27] Put simply, genes don't cause disease. Genes express themselves due to changes in our environment.

It has been established recently that more than 30 genes are responsible for breast cancer, so those companies that patented the rights to a single specific gene, thinking it was the only gene to cause a cancer, are not going to make the money they thought. The 'Human Genome Project,' in which every gene in a human body has been mapped, has not produced the Holy Grail everyone was expecting. Science is like that – no sooner do you discover something new than it delivers you the complete opposite as being true. Just look at Newtonian physics and Einstein's Theory of Relativity. Here you can find a great example of how science has changed the face of the earth as we know it.

I personally believe it is important that, while we explore what medicine has given us, we need to think again; we must ask some of the fundamental questions and not accept that what doctors tell us is always true. In Advanced Clearing Energetics, we are certain that people can die from a doctor's diagnosis. Not because of the doctors, who personally have the welfare of the patient at heart, but because of the way the patient's body reacts to both what the doctor says and the tone of voice used to say it. Just imagine what happens to a person who has just been told he or she has terminal cancer. A diagnosis such as this creates immense stress in a person, their family, work, and life. Everything has now changed: their environment, how they view life, how they view others, and subsequently the environment around their cells changes, causing many genes to change their expression and the possibility of further diseases to occur. Could this be the true cause of secondary cancers?

Doctors' beliefs and disease

Doctor's words are very powerful – a layperson saying the same thing about a prognosis for a patient doesn't have the same effect. The assumption that 'doctor knows best' has been handed down to us over many years. However, the tide is turning, because I believe the evidence they are using to substantiate their beliefs is out of date. Many doctors know this and have written extensively about a different shift in how they approach disease.

In 1986, Dr. Bernie Siegel, a US medical doctor, wrote the groundbreaking book *Love, Medicine and Miracles*, which suggested there was a direct link between how we perceive an illness, and our healing.[28] He used art therapy to understand and explain to patients how they were healing. This practice is still used today with great effect in places such as Penny Brohn Cancer Care in the UK (formerly the Bristol Cancer Help Centre). Furthermore, Dr. Siegel identified a major issue in conventional medical practice – the emotional trauma caused when a patient is given a diagnosis:

> *'Unfortunately doctors are not taught how to communicate with patients and so our words and the words given to patients to read induce negative side effects. The words are coming from an authority and have a hypnotic influence. They tell you all the things that can go wrong but do not tell you what can go right. So wordswordswords are swordswordswords. Yes, they become swords which can kill or cure as a scalpel can.'[29]*

The problem is that medical doctors who speak out in this way are often ostracized. The medical profession stops them from practicing by pushing them out of their positions, thereby making it impossible for them to practice inside the normal system. As a result, most doctors stick to the status quo, earn their money, and say nothing.

As you can probably guess, in most countries the medical profession can't move even if it wants to. It is stuck in a system that won't budge. However, people are starting to answer back. They are looking for alternatives and refusing to accept what the doctor says as true, quite often because the medical profession hasn't accepted the existence of what most of us know to be true: the mind–body link.

Furthermore, doctors still can't answer that elusive question: 'What causes disease?' They don't even know how placebos work. Yet they are totally aware of their presence. Drug companies are very perplexed that the mind (placebos via sugar pills) is as effective as the drugs in clinical trials.[30, 31] The placebo effect is not only related to drug treatment but also to surgery, demonstrated through a study into the effects of surgery on knees. Of three test groups, one test had no surgery, yet incisions were made in the patients' knees. This group recovered just as well as the other two groups, who did receive surgery.[32]

The role of fungi, bacteria, and viruses in disease

However, you may be asking the question: 'Aren't diseases due to fungi, bacteria, and viruses?' Here is something really fascinating: were you aware that before the infection expresses itself (e.g., you get a head cold), the virus is present in the blood system, multiplying but not active? Bacteria are multiplying in the blood long before the infection occurs. Before a fungal infection occurs, the fungus is growing, but again is dormant in the blood, ready to be used when it is required. We'll be discussing this in more depth in Chapter 9 (see page 187).

If disease is due to fungi, bacteria, and viruses, why do people rush to buy probiotic products that contain Lactobacillus casei Shirota bacteria? Why are these so-called good bacteria there? Surely we should kill all of them? Bacteria cause disease!

For example, we get food poisoning from bacteria, but why? Why doesn't everyone get food poisoning from the same meal? Why doesn't everyone get the flu when the flu is going around? Why doesn't everyone get athlete's foot when they go to the gym or swimming pool?

If these deadly fungi, bacteria, and viruses really did cause disease, then we would all be dead by now, because they are everywhere. You may say it's because you have a good immune system and antibodies to deal with these bugs. Well, I know plenty of healthy people who exercise, don't smoke, eat well, but at the first sight of a bug they become sick. There are also people who smoke, eat unhealthy food, and don't exercise, yet they never seem to get these infections. Why?

I've also met people who are at the pinnacle of health and fitness. They feel great, they look great, they exercise, they have great mental attitudes toward life, they eat all the right foods, and yet they get cancer, and are then told it is probably due to a virus, as in cervical cancer – the human papillomavirus (HPV). Why? Does this have anything to do with immunity? No, in Advanced Clearing Energetics we don't think it has.

Perhaps instead, viruses, bacteria, and fungi work in homeostasis (side by side) with our whole system as the cleaners and the digesters. Perhaps they are the workers of our body after we have been under stress.

There is also some evidence that so-called viruses such as smallpox and AIDS don't exist. No one has ever found the AIDS virus. In order to see a virus you need an incredibly powerful microscope. Only since the mid-1990s has the technology been available to do that. So how do we know these specific human viruses exist? And it gets worse: if these so-called viruses have been found and isolated so that vaccines can be developed, then how is it that no university in the world can prove they exist by producing a picture of them or by separating the virus structure completely outside of a cell? A brilliant virologist from Germany named Dr. Stefan Lanka isolated the first virus in seaweed and then started to study various pathogens only to discover that they were all fabricated. He even wrote to all the top medical universities asking them to prove that the viruses, which were being used as the basis for vaccinations, did exist. None of them to this day have ever been able to prove the existence of these viruses.[33]

I will explore this whole concept further in Chapter 9, but the theory that disease is due to fungi, bacteria, and viruses, again, like the other theories we have been sold, seems flawed. There is way more going on in the body than the medical profession and the pharmaceutical industry would lead you to believe.

Radiation, poison, toxins, and disease

You probably know that radiation kills. In the 1986 Chernobyl disaster, a nuclear reactor malfunctioned and resulted in a 640-mile exclusion zone. Studies show that the closer animals – mostly birds – lived to the center of the explosion, the more mutations occurred and birth rates were significantly suppressed. Further out, animals were less affected. However, the effects of the background radiation that fell from the skies internationally is thought to have affected 4,000 to 30,000 people worldwide, depending on which reports you read.[34] From the figures and observations, I think we can safely say that background radiation is not the cause of all disease. However, radiation in large dosages, as used in cancer treatments, can cause significant damage and even cancer, but the background amounts that we receive daily, in most healthy human beings, are not the cause of disease.

What about poisons? Yes, poisons do kill people, but a certain poison has to be administered in a certain quantity for it to have a damaging effect. Chemotherapy, derived from mustard gas – the same nerve agent used in World Wars I and II – is injected into cancer patients. Despite these extremely cytotoxic (toxic to cells) chemicals being used, the body can and does deal with high levels of poisons.

Any toxin in large qualities will kill you. In fact, any substance in large enough quantities or in the wrong place will kill you. Drinking too much water will kill you. Air injected into your veins will kill you. However, some people smoke and others live in poisonous environments, and some of these people survive with no side effects while others develop life-threatening diseases.

So the body can deal with a mass of toxins. The medical profession uses toxins and radiation to 'cure' cancer. Do toxins therefore cause disease? Yes, you can be poisoned. Yes, you can be exposed to a large amount of radiation and die from it. However, toxins are not the cause of all disease.

What are we left with?

The only thing that we haven't explored is stress within the environment. What I mean by 'the environment' is how we react to certain situations within our surroundings, other people, changing circumstances, challenging situations, which cause either immediate or ongoing stress that we can't deal with.

In the next chapter we'll explore this missing link in disease. What causes disease, pains, and ailments to occur, and where is the proof that this could be the case?

CHAPTER 3

WHAT CAUSES A DISEASE?

'Every human being is the author of their own health or disease.'

Buddha

We've already discussed many things relating to disease, including the fact that modern medicine has no idea what causes 99 percent of all diseases. This is rather alarming. How can you find a cure for something if you don't know what caused it?

The truth is that medical doctors can label a symptom very well. They are brilliant at emergency medicine, but they can't tell you why a disease occurs. They don't know, and as Isobel's story, on the next page, illustrates, not knowing the cause of a disease and therefore subscribing to the belief system that 'the body has made a mistake' has an influence on how a doctor treats a patient.

HEAD TUMOR – UNDERSTANDING THE WHOLE STORY

Isobel was a happy eight-year-old girl, full of life and completely normal, apart from a fist-sized tumor on her head. Her mother and stepfather took her to see a specialist, and a brain CT scan showed that the tumor wasn't connected to any part of the bone, nor was it invasive. However, the doctor was unable to explain the cause of the tumor and insisted that its quick removal was necessary to save the girl's life.

After the operation, Isobel recovered well and the tumor didn't regrow. But a month later, a PET (positron emission tomography) scan showed a small mark on her esophagus, which the doctor said was a secondary tumor. Her parents questioned whether the mark was caused from the tube inserted into her throat during the operation, as Isobel had been complaining of a pain in her lower throat since that time. Despite a second and third medical opinion to the contrary, the specialist refused to do more exploratory tests, and insisted on treating Isobel with nine months of chemotherapy.

Isobel became very sick during the treatment but slowly recovered; however, a few months later another scan showed the same unchanged marking on her esophagus. Another round of chemotherapy was ordered and she became very sick again. A few months later, the next scan showed the same marking in the same place; it hadn't changed. The doctor ordered exploratory surgery, which found scarring due to the tube inserted into her throat during the original surgery to remove the tumor.

Her mother and stepfather contacted me during this time, and I looked through Isobel's history and found the original shock conflict. Isobel had been hitting herself repeatedly on the head, which had caused the thin layer of skin surrounding the bones, called the periosteum, to break and the bone to thicken. The repeated hitting coupled with the rebuilding of the bone and the continual breaking of the periosteum resulted in the growth of the tumor. The reason for this behavior was her father (who had since divorced her mother and left the family home) repeatedly telling her she was stupid. In response, Isobel would hit herself, extremely hard, on her head if she got anything wrong.

Another medical doctor, who wasn't aware of Isobel's history until after he'd completed the CT scan reading, remarked that if the child had been left alone after surgery, there would have been no extra growth of the original tumor on her head. He also mentioned that there was no metastasis and, in the long term, if nothing further had been done, she would have made a full recovery. When told about the chemotherapy, he was horrified and said that this treatment was completely unnecessary, even in conventional medicine, especially after the PET scan had only shown the marking on the esophagus. A little more time spent on 'why' there was a dark spot on her esophagus would have saved her months of unnecessary chemotherapy.

It's impossible to know the consequences of the specialist's misdiagnosis on Isobel's long-term growth and health; chemotherapy is known to cause cancer and fertility problems, so only time will tell.

Fortunately, young people's bodies are very resilient, and Isobel's family was diligent in supporting her with homeopathy, nutritional changes, emotional support, and EFT along with detoxification programs after each treatment. Three years on, Isobel is a happy child again and, despite the emotional and physical trauma she experienced, she is thriving.

I've come across many people with similar problems and experienced them myself, too. My guess is that it's likely you also either know someone or experienced something similar yourself. But if you don't know the cause of the problem, then how can you solve it?

When I asked a medical doctor how the drugs worked to cure gastric flu, I was told: 'The pills didn't cure you, your body does that naturally, and the drugs merely block you up. Most drugs just mask your symptoms while your body heals itself.'

So how can doctors work if they don't know what causes a disease to occur? To understand this we need to go back to the beginnings of the medical profession.

Over 200 years ago, when doctors first started practicing medicine, they were considered quacks. People believed in religion more than doctors. Doctors were members of the Royal College of Barbers and Surgeons, but in 1745 they broke away, as they had started to earn more money and gain respect. Modern medicine only really started to make a difference in people's health after the introduction of Louis Pasteur's 'germ' theory in the late nineteenth century, when doctors first began to understand that germs were a cause of disease and death.

Germs do have a part to play in death. There is no doubt that cleanliness reduces the likelihood of dying from a horrible infection, but why? After all, these germs are already in our system and we live in symbiosis with them. They only become active during certain times and only for a reason.

Since then, very little has changed, and the theory that disease is due to germs has been the major premise behind modern medicine's approach to healing, even with the introduction of new diagnostic machines, such as computer tomography (CT's, 1973), ultrasound (1979), and magnetic resonance imaging (MRI, 1977). Diagnosis is still a haphazard process.

HEART PROBLEMS – MISDIAGNOSIS

Robert's father wasn't in good health, but the doctors didn't know why, and matters became much more serious when he suffered a cardiac arrest. He received CPR from Robert before the ambulance arrived and rushed him to hospital, where he was diagnosed with coronary heart disease and given a cocktail of drugs followed by an operation.

Robert isn't a doctor, but he does have a vast amount of medical knowledge and, having cared for his father at home, thought his father's symptoms didn't fit with the hospital's diagnosis of coronary heart disease; instead he believed they pointed to a disease of the heart muscles. His opinions, however, were brushed aside by the hospital.

A month after the cardiac arrest, his father died, and Robert was grief-stricken but also angry because on postmortem, his death was found to be due not to his heart condition but to pneumonia, which was misdiagnosed while he was in the hospital.

If you consider Robert's father's death and Isobel's experience to be rare occurrences, then you might be surprised to learn that according to a Bloomberg report, 'Death by Medicine,' released by the Nutritional Institute of Medicine in 2004, the number one cause of death in the USA is the medical system itself: 'A definitive review and close reading of medical peer-review journals and government health statistics shows that American medicine frequently causes more harm than good.'[1]

Since Edward Jenner's discovery of the first vaccine and Louis Pasteur's germ theory, modern medicine has seemingly remained unchanged regarding the cause of disease; in other words, the cause of most disease is unknown. Furthermore, only 100 bacteria have been identified as having a detrimental effect on our bodies (see also page 190).

Take cardiovascular disease, for example. The medical profession doesn't know what causes it, but they have established risk factors, e.g., high blood pressure, high cholesterol, diabetes, obesity, smoking, stress, alcohol, and age, which indicate those people who are more likely to get the disease.

Now I agree that people with these risk factors are more likely to develop some form of heart issue, but what causes cardiovascular diseases to occur? There are people with one or all of these risk factors who never develop heart problems, and there are others who don't have any of these issues but who do have heart problems. Why? What caused them to develop these problems? The medical profession cannot explain this.

What about cancer? What causes cancer? A defective gene? A virus? A bacterium? Old age? Your immune system? Diet? Carcinogens? Your environment? The medical profession does not know.

You can find a complete list of all the things, according to epidemiologists, that give you cancer. Looking through the list I realize I should not be alive. And neither should you. Here's the shortened list:

Alcohol, air pollution, aspartame, baby food, barbecued meat, bottled water, bracken, bread, breasts, bus stations, casual sex, exhaust fumes, celery, cell (mobile) phones, charred foods, chewing gum, Chinese food, chips (crisps), chlorinated water, cholesterol, low cholesterol, chromium, coal tar, coffee, coke ovens, crackers, creosote, dairy products, deodorants, depression, diesel exhaust, diet soda, estrogen, fat, fluoridation, flying, formaldehyde, French fries, fruit, gasoline, genes, gingerbread, global warming, granite, grilled meat, hair dyes, hamburgers, high bone mass, hydrogen peroxide, incense, infertility, jewelry, kissing, lack of exercise, laxatives, lead, left-handedness, low-fiber diet, magnetic fields, marijuana, microwave ovens, milk hormones, mixed spices, night lighting, night shifts, not breast feeding, not having a twin, nuclear power plants, obesity, olestra, olive oil, orange juice, oyster sauce, ozone, ozone depletion, passive smoking, PCBs, peanuts, pesticides, pet birds, plastic IV bags, power lines, proteins, PVC, radio masts, railway sleepers, red meat, saccharin, salt, semiconductor plants, shellfish, sick building syndrome, soy sauce, stress, styrene, sulphuric acid, sunbeds, sunlight, sunscreen, talcum powder, testosterone, tight bras, toast, toasters, tobacco, tooth fillings, toothpaste (with fluoride or bleach), train stations, underarm shaving, unvented stoves, UV radiation, vegetables, vinyl toys, vitamins, wallpaper, welding fumes, well water, weight gain, winter, wood dust, work, x-rays.[2]

Even after taking out all the chemical names, this list is still ridiculous.

We've already established that the medical profession can't say what causes cancer or heart disease (the two biggest killers), but they also don't know what causes any of the following common diseases:

◉ Multiple sclerosis (MS)

◉ Eczema

◉ Irritable Bowel Syndrome (IBS)

◉ Acne

◉ Depression

◉ Ovarian cysts

◉ Prostate cancer

◉ Diabetes type II

We do know, however, that almost every major illness is linked to chronic stress, and this was also the conclusion of a research paper by Segerstrom and Miller in 2004[3] and many others since 1999.[4, 5, 6]

Stress: the missing cause

In Advanced Clearing Energetics we have an answer to the question of 'what causes disease?' Experience of working with clients with all of the diseases listed above (including cancer and heart disease) shows that when people go through a shocking experience that they are unable to deal with, it causes the body to change, freeze, fight, or defend itself. The criteria of the shock must be as follows:

Unexpected
Dramatic
Isolating
No strategy

All of the criteria, which I call UDIN for ease of reference, must be present for a disease to occur. Let me explain each one:

Unexpected

An **unexpected** shock comes out of the blue. For example, parents see their child killed by a speeding car, or the sudden loss of a parent or loved one at a young age. On the other hand, if parents frequently tell their child (or vice versa) they will commit suicide, then if they do, it is a traumatic shock but not unexpected. There was 'an expectation' this could happen.

Dramatic

A **dramatic** shock means there is a lot of emotional energy involved in the event. An example would be the decision to end a destructive relationship despite loving the other person. Hearing the voice of a partner pleading can hurt very deeply. An unexpected shock that is not that dramatic might be overhearing some unwelcome news, such as parents learning that their son or daughter plans to spend Christmas with their partner rather than with them because the parents don't get along with the partner.

Isolating

An **isolating** shock means feeling totally alone in dealing with the event. Having to fight to stay in the marital home after the death of a partner or spouse, because children want the home to be sold, would be an example. An unexpected, dramatic shock, which is not isolating, is where the trauma is a shared experience. For example, an entire class mourning the loss of a classmate killed in a car accident; everyone talks openly about their feelings of grief.

No strategy

A shock where a person has **no strategy** is one where an incident happens but people have no idea what to do to resolve the situation. They are lost in the wilderness and rerun the event again and again, trying to find a way out of it. An example might be being wrongly accused of adultery by a close friend, who refuses to listen to reason. On the other hand, being fired for a fictional misdemeanor by a vindictive boss is unexpected, dramatic, and isolating, but the employment laws provide a strategy to resolve this type of situation.

BREAST CANCER – AN INABILITY TO NURTURE

I met Jenny through Peter Fraser, who was working with her using the NES system. Jenny had been diagnosed with breast cancer two years earlier and had been fighting it ever since. She'd received chemotherapy, but was so sick from it that it almost killed her. Her oncologist said that he'd never seen anyone react to chemotherapy in that way.

However, when she came to see me she seemed full of health, life, and vitality. She'd refused further chemotherapy and had made a decision to try alternative approaches. The questions she wanted me to answer were: why did she get cancer, what was the cause, and why did it happen at that time in her life?

When she sent me her history, I saw what might have caused her issue: it was a shock to do with her son. Jenny's first husband was a very unpleasant man, but she became pregnant and trapped in the relationship. It was so difficult that she made a massive sacrifice: to leave her husband and her children.

Jenny's life was difficult and she had many problems, but her main issue was that her son was a heroin addict. One day he called her out of the blue to say that he had been arrested for raping a girl. Jenny told me how the sound of his voice was so chilling that it still resonated deep inside her.

As I probed further into the circumstances around this phone call, Jenny went bright red and relived the shock of hearing his voice saying how helpless he was. Her son didn't know what to do. He didn't even know if he had raped the girl and was facing a long prison sentence if found guilty. Jenny told me how she felt a massive fear that she might never see him again.

This event changed her whole life. She dropped everything she was doing and started a one-woman crusade to clear her son's name. Eventually, Jenny succeeded, and you could hear the relief in her voice

WHY AM I SICK?

as she recounted the 'not guilty' verdict delivered by the jury.

However, her son didn't seem to care less; it was almost as if he was glad that he'd been arrested so that she had to save him. He didn't care that she'd spent all her money and every moment of her time to clear his name. After leaving prison he went straight back to using heroin again.

It made me very sad to hear that Jenny didn't survive her cancer. She had a problem with swallowing and eventually had to go to hospital to become rehydrated and needed a feeding tube. While she was in the hospital, a full body CT scan found bone, liver, and lung cancer, which had been there for some time, maybe years. After hearing this news, her loving husband, Brian, told me, she very quickly gave up on life.

Jenny was a fighter, and I hope that her story will assist others in understanding what really causes a disease, something I will explain in more detail in the following chapters. She showed great resilience to try other forms of therapies after chemotherapy, and it is possible that NES and intensive dietary changes kept her alive, way beyond the medical prognosis.

Advanced Clearing Energetics – what causes a disease?

So from an Advanced Clearing Energetics point of view, the cause of disease is trapped energy in the system or, as Karl Dawson calls it, 'the Matrix.' Triggered by a specific stressful

UDIN event, the body changes – to freeze, fight, or defend itself – and in doing so creates disease.

Bruce Lipton explains in *The Biology of Belief* that a cell changes its constitution based on its surroundings. When under stressful situations, a cell is working. When there is no stress, the cell regenerates. There are two states to how a cell reacts, and it cannot be in a stressed state and repairing itself at the same time.[7] What we are interested in, however, is the stress. If the event is unexpected, dramatic, isolating, and there is no strategy to deal with it, then the cell remains in an ongoing stressful state. It doesn't have a chance to repair itself.

If our environment suddenly changes and we don't know what to do, we have a UDIN shock, where the cells in specific organs change their structure and function. Similarly, we also know that when a person gets an illness/disease, it doesn't affect every organ; a person gets breast or bowel cancer, eczema, muscle wastage, a cough, etc. The illness/disease is localized.

As I've explained, research has scientifically proven that a cell changes its function and structure as a result of changes in environmental conditions. We are also aware that almost every major illness that people acquire is linked to chronic stress. If the illnesses/diseases are localized in one part of an organ in the body, then why are the cells in those organs changing? For this we need to look at some basic biology.

Body functions and disease

Let's look at some of the organs and their basic functions, and how they respond to a disease or stressful event.

Digestive tract

A disease in this part of the body indicates an inability to digest something that has become stuck. If you can't digest a piece of food, then the food behind won't be digested either because it is unable to move down the digestive tract. The functioning and possible survival of the organism is threatened; if it cannot eat, it will starve. The cells in that part of the digestive tract change their structure and function, so they are able to digest the food that's stuck more effectively.

This can be seen in worms. If a piece of food becomes stuck in the digestive tract, more digestive tract is created around the area where the food is stuck. More digestive juices are produced from the new surrounding cells, and the chunk of food is digested and then pushed up or out of the organism. As this happens, the excess cells that were created are pushed out.

The specific localized cells change due to the stress of the stuck food so that the body can eliminate the problem and carry on digesting food to ensure survival. In humans, information is food. Information affects our livelihood. Suddenly finding out that one's life savings had been lost due to poor financial advice could be an example.

Glands and breasts

During pregnancy, cells change their function in the mammary glands in response to hormonal changes in the woman's body; the breasts grow bigger to produce milk to nurture the baby. The mother's inherent knowledge that the baby's survival depends on her milk in its first few months outside of the womb causes the localized cells in the breast glands to multiply. The breasts are a point of nurture in a woman, as they are there literally to feed a newborn baby. In the wild, without this food the baby would die. The extra growth of breast tissue is a natural female biological response, one that every pregnant mother has experienced.

Bones and muscles

If a bone is broken, then the body naturally mends it. In the wild, an animal with a broken back leg will often survive the trauma and be walking on the leg within six weeks, without help from man. After the stress of a bone being broken, the cells change to rebuild it. The cells organize themselves in an amazing way, rebuilding the bone in exactly the right amount in the right place. A strange phenomenon that any orthopedic doctor would verify is that the rebuilt bone is stronger than the original bone in humans and animals alike.

When you tear a muscle during intense exercise, it rebuilds itself to be stronger and bigger than before. Body-builders know this to be true, as their whole profession is based on this natural fact.

Skin

During eczema there is a loss of skin followed by rebuilding. Medical professionals usually treat eczema with steroid creams, which thin and desensitize the skin rather than cure the problem. However, the skin is our tactile sensory organ, which connects us to our loved ones. The desensitized skin prevents a person from feeling that missing touch; you don't think about the person you've lost contact with.

The rebuilding stage of eczema is the red, hot, and itchy rash that appears, but anyone who suffers from the condition knows there are two parts: the light, scaly, desensitized, cold skin and then a red, very sensitive, itchy, hot skin. When some mothers switch from breast to formula feeding, some babies will get eczema on their cheeks. The medical profession says this is an allergic reaction to the formula. Could it instead be the loss of contact between the baby and the mother's breast?

From what we know about stress causing disease and the cells' function changing to adapt to environmental conditions, eczema is due to the loss of skin-to-skin contact. This is a far more plausible answer, particularly as the medical profession is unable to fully explain what causes the allergy.

A simple theory

From an Advanced Clearing Energetics perspective, as the UDIN shock happens, a chain of unconscious reactions determine our response to it, and the body makes specific choices as to which organ will be affected. This is determined by the content of the shock and basic biology.

As I mentioned earlier, if the issue is an inability to nurture, then it affects the breast. An issue concerning the skin would be the result of a loss of contact. A gut issue would be related to something that cannot be digested; and an issue to do with the muscles would be because we don't feel strong enough, perhaps, to fight back.

So a UDIN shock doesn't affect every organ in the body, just the one that is connected to that specific type of shocking event. There is also a corresponding reaction in the brain, which can be seen as a ring on a brain CT scan. Using embryology (see also page 167), each one of these 'shocks' shows up in the location in the brain that is directly related to the affected organ. Recent research also shows that the shock is picked up by the heart energies several seconds before it shows up in the brain or another organ.

According to Peter Fraser of NES Health, the heart is not just a pump but also imprints the blood with important information to share with every organ. It also sends out a wave of information into the world magnetically and energetically.[8] I believe that this energetic imprinting also puts us in specific situations and attracts certain individuals to us.

In addition, Peter Fraser describes how these shocks in the brain and organs resonate at the same frequency as the waves used in CT scanning (i.e., x-rays). Therefore, you can see these UDIN shocks stored in specific locations. Further research is required, but I would suggest that these shocks are likely to be the same trapped energetic imprints that cause disease.

This theory certainly fits with my experience. When I work with resolving emotional conflicts, I find that people often get headaches at the exact point of the ring on their CT scan, even after they've released the issue. Chapter 8 is dedicated to the brain and the location of these rings (if you would like to see examples and pictures of CT scans, visit www.whyamisick.com).

Even more recently I've discovered that the UDIN shock is picked up immediately by the heart and a message sent to the brain and also the gut. The gut assesses and measures the shock emotionally; and this theory seems to be corroborated by recent research into the gut, which indicates it is, in fact, intelligent and can be considered to be a second brain.[9]

Symptoms following a shock

As the shock happens, the body also changes its state from a normal everyday waking state into a state of stress, typically called the fight, flight, or freeze response. This is an ancient inbuilt response designed to enable us to cope in a suddenly hostile environment e.g., fighting tigers or bears.

Typical symptoms are cold extremities – your hands, feet, and skin feel cold. There is a rush of energy in the form of adrenalin to your heart, which beats faster. You feel wide awake, wired, and full of energy. Your focus and attention is on one thing and one thing only – the stressful event you're going through and what you can do to solve it or get out of it.

Also, during this time, your personality changes. What you see, hear, feel, taste, and smell is affected. Your unconscious mind filters out what it doesn't need and draws attention to what it wants to focus on, often as an avoidance system.

Also, our filters change and our personality is altered to solve the problem. The UDIN event is imprinted into specific places in the corresponding organ and the brain, our guts also store the emotion from the event, and our heart sends out a different message to our body and its surroundings. It seems our body becomes obsessed, almost like a machine, with one aim – to solve the problem.

Poisoning, accidents, and malnutrition are also shocks in their own right. Malnutrition, when it gets to a critical stage, causes a shock to the body and starts to shut off specific organs one by one.

So, we understand that it is very likely that a specific type of shock is the cause of a disease. The evidence seems to point in that direction. This is also evident through our use of language. Here are some examples taken from clients who experienced these issues.

- ◉ 'It hit me in the pit of my stomach' – stomach ulcer.
- ◉ 'It stuck in my throat' – losing your voice.
- ◉ 'It totally stank' – sinusitis.
- ◉ 'I was being attacked head on' – pleurisy.
- ◉ 'I felt powerless' – hypothyroidism.
- ◉ 'It broke my heart' – heart disease.
- ◉ 'It was as if an arrow had pierced right through me' – melanoma.
- ◉ 'I was crippled by what was said' – herniated disc.
- ◉ 'I was so shocked I couldn't even come up for air' – bronchial asthma.
- ◉ 'I feel so totally disconnected from everyone' – eczema.
- ◉ 'The sweetness drained right out of my life' – diabetes.

In my work with clients, finding the shock that started the disease process is profound. It answers the question of why the disease is there and explains the symptoms to the client. I can describe exactly how clients' personalities changed, and how they reacted to other people and situations after the shock. It is as if I'm reading their horoscopes, only there's no guesswork, no hypothesis on my part. I'm using theory to do this.

From an Advanced Clearing Energetics perspective, the UDIN, the shocking experience, is the key to unlocking why a disease is there and what the body does following this event.

In the next chapter, we'll discuss how, during this shock, the brain, organ, and heart connection is affected, as well as how that changes our whole environment and social behavior. This explains so much about why our world changes after a UDIN and how we also change personality, something I only touched upon in this chapter.

CHAPTER 4

DISEASE AFFECTS EVERYTHING

'I would feel more optimistic about a bright future for man if he spent less time proving that he can outwit Nature and more time tasting her sweetness and respecting her seniority.'

E.B. White, American writer

When you think about it, the role that changes in the brain, organs, heart, behavior, and environment play in our lives after a shock is astounding. There is so much more going on than just the physical symptoms.

The mind-body-spirit connection is amazing, and when we add behavioral and environmental conditions, then we see that everything is interlinked into one elegant, magnificent system. We see that disease is not a mistake, but a fantastic massive program, each part linked to the original trapped energetic imprint, which leads back to the stressful UDIN event that caused the body to go into a spin.

So far I've talked about serious diseases in much of this book; however, Sam's ear infections were not life-threatening, yet the effect of the issue on his life was overwhelming.

EAR PROBLEMS – INABILITY TO TRUST

Sam is a great guy. He works really hard traveling around the country constructing stages for large concerts. Although he doesn't like his work, he's the foreman, and well liked by his workmates because he has a reputation for staying calm even when things are going completely wrong. He also runs and plays in a successful band.

When he came to see me, Sam wanted to be coached using NLP. But during our sessions he kept complaining that he didn't trust anyone, including himself. Realizing that Advanced Clearing Energetics could help him, I asked whether he'd had any illnesses in the past few months. He nonchalantly replied that he had ear infections in both ears. He was taking antibiotics, which were having no effect whatsoever, and one ear was worse than the other.

I asked him what had been going on in his life a month prior to the ear infections. He told me that he and his girlfriend had had some 'issues,' which were affecting their relationship, and she'd told him to leave her alone. Alarmed and upset by the breakdown of the relationship, Sam moved to a friend's house; but the two argued, and his friend had said some really hurtful things to him during the argument.

All in all, Sam had heard two alarming things within the space of a few weeks. He told me that he felt continually stressed for a while and then settled down a bit, but things weren't right, and this was the real reason he started coming to see me.

He also said that during this time his calm personality had changed. He lost touch with his girlfriend who he really wanted to be with and loved; however, he felt he couldn't trust her, and even accused her of being unfaithful. Band members were also a problem, and everything seemed to be falling apart around him. His work was terrible, he kept arguing with everyone, and subsequently wanted to quit.

When I explained the link between the two alarming events, his ear infections and his behavior, Sam was speechless. I told him he literally 'could not believe what he was hearing.' He was in a strange no-man's-land: knowing why he had the problem, believing what I was saying and recognizing all the changes that had happened to him, yet he could not trust himself or me. I even did a demonstration of how he would behave with other people, and he confirmed that this was how he reacted. Knowing that he would never trust himself or me, I just moved on and did the therapy.

This involved taking both the stressful incidents and the two people who had caused them, and placing them on Sam's opposite hands. Then I spoke to both people, who metaphorically were on his left and right hands, and slowly brought his hands together. There was a massive shift in Sam: he was at a loss for words and his body became really hot. After this, his whole energy changed, and a few minutes later he said: 'That was very weird, but I feel different; I feel normal again,' and I could see that a calmness had come over him.

Two weeks later everything had shifted for Sam. He and his girlfriend resolved their issues and moved in together. The situation with his work returned to normal, and he felt happier inside. The friend apologized for being so unpleasant. The band members stopped arguing with him. I have since periodically met up with Sam, and these days he's always happy and cheerful, and life is treating him very well. His ears also cleared up without continuing the antibiotics.

For me, the true significance and moral of this story was in the understanding of the massive effect that stressful events can have on everything in our lives. They don't just change the body; they also change the brain, the organs, the heart, our behavior, and our environment. All are altered and, by working back from one symptom, whether it is psychological, environmental, or physical, we can determine which stressful event caused everything to change in the first place.

In traditional medicine, there is neither a link between the mind and the body, nor is there a connection to behavior or the environment. If there were, then doctors wouldn't administer so many drugs because they would realize the effect the drugs have on people's minds, which in turn affect their environment and actions.

A doctor's manner of giving a diagnosis to a patient can also be as detrimental to the patient's recovery as the disease itself, and this is particularly true in life-threatening illnesses, such as cancer. The problem is that most doctors are not trained in having a good bedside manner. Furthermore, they simply don't have time to worry about their patients' emotions, and I'm certain that most doctors have little or no idea how much of an influence they have on their patients.

I often find that I have to coach my clients through every word a doctor has said to them. Some people react as if they are in a hypnotic trance when in front of a doctor and take every word as the truth.

In one very sad case, I had a client who was diagnosed with lymphatic cancer. Little did the oncologist know that this patient had always believed she would die of cancer. When I interviewed her a few weeks after the diagnosis, she told me that when she heard the word 'cancer,' she went white inside and knew she was going to die. The doctor told her this type of cancer was treatable and the prognosis was good, but all she heard was that she had cancer. Her mother had died of cancer, and she believed she would, too.

After a few weeks she was called for further tests, and this time the oncologist found dark spots on her lungs, not present before. The cancer was a single-cell carcinoma – a very aggressive, inoperable bronchial lung cancer. She was given a month to live without chemotherapy, six months with, but she refused treatment and died a morphine-induced death within a month, just as the doctor predicted.

Fearing one's death can cause a single-cell carcinoma to occur. The reason the body does this is to allow the person more air to travel into the lungs, adding more oxygen to the blood, allowing the person to be able to fight the impending death threat. The black spots on the lungs are extra cells grown by the body in a last-ditch attempt to deal with the death threat.

Dr. Bernie Siegel, the well-known American oncologist, explains the importance of diagnosis in his book *Love, Medicine and Miracles* (1986):

'The way a doctor works with a client is vitally important.
The clients are in a highly vulnerable state when they are
presented with the information that could mean life or death,
and that tells them how the symptoms of a disease are going
to play out. Many doctors use statistics to explain a cancer
prognosis. Telling the client that they have a one in five
chance of surviving (meaning their chances are very slim), is
how they put the data across. However, who is to know that
the client might be in the 20 percent that survive? How a
person hears the information is so important.'

How the body reacts to a UDIN

Any event that has a lot of stress behind it causes the body
to react in a way to support it through the issue. We know
this from the previous chapter. What is not clear is that when
we experience a stressful event, an Unexpected, Dramatic,
Isolating event where we have No strategy for dealing with
the experience (UDIN), it affects us in many ways, not just
physically. Normally, we're unaware of what is happening to
us physically after the stress hits, but what we can notice are
other effects, which show up on multiple levels. All together
we see that our brain, specific organs, heart, behavior, and
environment are affected by a UDIN.

Brain

Here we see trapped energy in the form of rings appearing
in the brain at a specific location based on embryology,
observed via brain CT scans. This is relative to the type of
shock that has occurred. It also relates to the organ best
designed to support the individual through that particular
issue. What happens in the brain can change brain chemistry,

manifesting as anxiety, paranoia, depression, or mania. Other psychosomatic issues may also occur due to this imbalance. So we can say that there is a personality change that occurs in the person, relative to the brain chemistry and the conflict shock.

Organ

In the body, a specific organ reacts in line with the shock – e.g., part of the bowel grows in the Stress Stage of the disease (see page 91) or there is a necrosis, as in muscle wastage. The organ changes to support the whole person through the UDIN. After the UDIN has been addressed, which may not always happen, the organ needs to repair itself. Often this stage of the process is painful, involves swelling, and a significant alteration of the function of the organ involved.

Heart

The overall spirit of the person is affected, through the actions of the heart. As I explained in Chapter 3, the heart imprints the blood with information with every beat, and that tells every organ in the body what is going on energetically. It is also sending out a magnetic wave, putting people in different environmental surroundings and introducing them to other people so that they can solve the shock.

Behavior

People will change their way of behaving with other people so they can find a solution to the shock; the heart is influencing these decisions. If there is a specific individual who was there at the time of the original stressful event, then how that person reacts around that individual will change in accordance with the problem. (This could also be a group of individuals, e.g., family or work colleagues).

Environment

What we do and where we go, or what we're attracted to, are integrated into the whole process. The way a person reacts with regard to a specific area, place, or item is affected during the stressful event. For example, if people were shocked while working at their office desks, then that environment becomes linked at the unconscious level, and returning to that place can trigger the whole stressful feeling again. (This explains chronic diseases and allergies.)

How disease plays out

Let me give you an example. One of my students, Lucille, a very lovable woman with a great sense of humor, suffered with anxiety all of her life. In Advanced Clearing Energetics terms, anxiety is due to multiple shocks that affect the thyroglossal ducts and the pharyngeal gland.

Lucille confirmed that throughout her life she'd suffered from anxiety and was able to identify two separate UDIN moments: her violent father punching her mother in the womb while she was carrying Lucille, and then her father forcing himself upon her mother in a rage of drunken jealousy. These specific shocks affected the pharyngeal gland and the thyroid (thyroglossal ducts) and showed up as two rings in the frontal lobes on her brain CT scan (to see Lucille's brain CT scan, visit www.whyamisick.com). Lucille remembered feeling totally powerless during these shocks. She could do nothing, and her body reacted by altering the way the thyroid (an endocrine gland) functions.

Under stress there is a cell necrosis (cell removal), which causes the amount of thyroxin pumped into the blood to increase. This is called hyperthyroidism. The body's reason for doing this is so that people are better able to deal with the thing they feel powerless against; they can react faster. However, ongoing excessive thyroxin in the system makes them feel continually anxious. And the change in the pharyngeal gland causes the body to absorb more oxygen into the blood, the net effect being that the person has more fight-or-flight energy.

Lucille's whole life had been affected by this major incident in the five different areas:

Brain

Two rings in the frontal lobes of Lucille's brain CT scan (cortex). This combination of thyroid (thyroglossal ducts) and pharyngeal gland is known to mean the person will suffer from ongoing anxiety. She also experienced tightness in the forehead and regular headaches in this area.

Organ

Lucille's body had too much thyroxin in it, and she felt continually anxious. The ducts of the thyroid gland increased in size, therefore allowing more thyroxin to be pumped into the blood quickly for a faster response. And the pharyngeal gland allows greater absorption of oxygen into the blood, causing the person to be able to respond faster.

Heart

The heart was sending out a message to the people around Lucille that attracted her to men and situations that were similar to the one she had experienced. Consequently, she had long-term relationships with abusive, violent men; and this was due to trying to resolve at a very deep level the issue she had experienced with her father as a child. The strange thing was, Lucille loved all these men because every one of them had forced themselves upon her. That's how she experienced love, and that's how the associations from childhood had become linked.

Behavior
She had rejected many other men that she found physically attractive because she never felt love toward them. She only went out with men in long-term relationships who, unconsciously for her, replayed the same original shock.

Environment
She moved to the UK to get away from her past in South Africa and worked at meaningless jobs because she felt powerless to do anything that would put her in the spotlight. She is an intelligent woman, but had low self-esteem and took recreational drugs to alter her mood.

All symptoms are interlinked
The really interesting thing about this way of thinking using Advanced Clearing Energetics is that the body is a metaphor for what is happening on an energetic level. If you only know certain specific symptoms from each one of these areas, you can clearly see that everything else is interlinked. As an example, let's take someone with eczema on both inner arms. We can compile a lot of the details relating to the other five areas:

Brain

There will be two rings in the outer cortex of the brain, near the center of the top of the head. People will have regular experiences of feeling blanked out, as the whole process of the eczema goes through its stages. They may experience headaches or pressure on the top of their heads from time to time.

Organ

The eczema will flare up after going through a stressful period. It will probably have shown up on the left and right arms in childhood whenever they experienced a separation issue with their parents (e.g., father or mother being away).

Heart

During the separation, they would have times of not caring about others followed by times of wanting to be in touch with friends and family. There would be an ongoing issue of being separated from people to whom they feel connected. There would be problems with personal relationships. They would find it very difficult to let go of a partner, and separations would involve a lot of drama. Essentially there would have been a UDIN shock in which the mother and father separated abruptly, perhaps a divorce or forced separation due to work or other issues.

Behavior

The faces of certain partners would trigger off the Stress Stage of the eczema (we'll discuss the stages of disease in the next chapter); this would probably occur during arguments, or at times when the other party would be away for certain lengths of time. Most likely a particular tone of voice used by a partner would trigger off the Stress Stage of the eczema. Generally they will be tactile people in nature and want to hold others close.

Environment

Specific objects, pictures, or places would trigger the Stress Stage of the eczema: e.g., a ticking clock, a family picture, walking past the old family home, or an ex-partner's house.

Even though this is a fictional example, my experience with working with eczema sufferers means that these links in all the five areas are accurate. When a UDIN occurs, it affects every part of the person – in a completely holistic way. The mind and body are not separate entities. Everything works as a whole integrated unit; everything is connected.

Knowing this means that we can no longer simply treat the body chemistry with a pill to solve a problem. We need to look at all the other aspects of a person in order to solve the root cause of an issue – if that person is to get well and stay well.

Body communication

The mind–body connection is not new-found knowledge. It is well understood by scientists that neurotransmitters (special chemicals that neurons use to communicate with each other) bathe every single cell in the body. When you have a thought, every cell in the body, from your big toe up to the cell in the end of your earlobe, is aware of it. We even know that as the heart beats, it imprints the blood with information telling every cell in the body what has happened, is happening, and may yet happen. This information is also being transmitted, via the electromagnetic field created by the heart, to attract certain people to us and to place us in specific situations to enable us to solve the UDIN. Our body communicates in a quantum mechanical way. In other words, imagine the nerve connections within a group of nerve cells in the body as being like the alphabet. As Bruce Lipton describes in his book *The Biology of Belief*, we don't have a neat string of connections that follow each other in a linear way – A then B then C, and so on (*see below*). Instead, A, B, C, D, E, etc., are all interconnected as one (*see bottom*).

A→B→C→D→E

Newtonian way – the linear approach

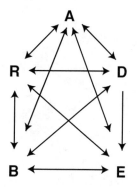

Quantum way – the holistic/interconnected approach[1]

The holistic model explains why many drugs don't work in the way they are expected to work, because in reality so much more is going on. Although quantum physics has been around since the early part of the twentieth century, and every cell in the body works in a quantum way, the medical profession and the pharmaceutical industry have ignored this fact completely. They still have very little idea why drugs have the side effects they do, or placebos work as well as, and in some instances better than, the original drug. Candace Pert's book *Molecules of Emotion* explains how thoughts and emotions affect our health.[2] Are our bodies and minds distinct from one another, or do they function together as part of an interconnected system?

In the next chapter, we'll explore further how the mind–body connection works in an incredible way by showing symptoms at specific times, based on a program that has six stages with two distinct parts: a warm and a cold part. These stages are undeniable when you see them in action, and their implications for all of medicine are profound. This next piece is fundamental to Advanced Clearing Energetics.

CHAPTER 5

THE SIX STAGES OF DISEASE

'Sometimes, if you stand on the bottom rail of a bridge and lean over to watch the river slipping slowly away beneath you, you will suddenly know everything there is to be known.'

A.A. Milne, English writer and creator of Winnie the Pooh

We know disease is caused by a UDIN, but what happens next? Why do we get symptoms of pain, disease, or fever? Could there be a process that the body follows in creating disease? Could it be so obvious that once you notice it, you'll ask yourself, 'How could I have missed that?' More important, how could the medical profession miss it? I think the next story about an ulcerated larynx will open your eyes; there's a twist at the end.

ULCERATED LARYNX – A NATURAL RESOLUTION TO STRESS

A friend came to me and reported that she had recently been laid up in bed and wanted to know why.

She was working on a very stressful project and was blamed by her boss for something she didn't do. She spent a lot of time obsessing about the repercussions of this and was scared.

For a week she worked really hard and didn't sleep well. She went to bed late and woke up very early each morning, and took work home with her to try to solve the problem. She obsessed about who had caused her boss to blame her for this problem. Even with the small amount of sleep she was getting, she felt fine and said she was ready to take on the world. She told me her workouts at the gym were the best she had done in a long while.

A week later, after working out who was responsible for the problem at work, the issue was resolved. Her boss apologized to her and she no longer felt scared. A few hours later, she felt her throat becoming uncomfortable, and over the next few hours she started to lose her voice. She didn't feel well, so she left work earlier than usual, got home, went to bed early, and slept very deeply. She stayed off work for a few days and rested. But three days later, she got out of bed early feeling much better. She went to work, but by midday she felt unwell again. Her symptoms had returned and she felt exhausted, which left her no choice but to leave work and go back to bed. A few days after that, everything returned to normal.

I explained to her that being blamed for the problem at work was a UDIN shock. She was stressed and her larynx membranes became ulcerated and widened; she wasn't aware of these physical changes, but biologically it allowed her *faster inhalation of air, and therefore she had more energy to solve the problem.*

When her boss apologized, however, the need for more air and energy disappeared, but the ulceration needed to be repaired. During the stressful time, a virus had collected in the blood. At exactly the same time that her boss apologized to her, the virus, working with the brain and body, started to repair the ulcerated laryngeal membranes. The body's energy switched from fight/flight to repairing itself. She got hot, sweaty, tired, felt ill, and ached all over. You can't do anything else but rest during this time. There was an increase of secretion from the repairing mucous membranes of the larynx, which made her cough, her voice became deeper and constrained, her energy reserves went into healing, and the obsession stopped.

This, I explained, is what we call 'the common cold or a cough.' She laughed, saying, 'I didn't realize the common cold could be that amazing.'

It's worth noting, also, that some people get bronchial colds not laryngeal ones, which is why it's called a chest cold. This happens to men more often than women and is due to how differently our brains are wired. If we get a nasal cold (head cold), it's because something has gotten up our nose. We can get combinations of all three colds.

In order to really understand what is happening here we need to delve into the wonderful world of our nervous system. The six stages of a disease are managed first by the sympathetic nervous system, and then by the parasympathetic nervous system.

Sympathetic nervous system

After a UDIN shock occurs, the body reacts to support us so that we can deal with the issue we were confronted with; it activates the 'sympathetic' nervous system, which appears as:

- Stress, tense body

- Obsessive thinking

- Sleeplessness

- Absence of appetite

- Weight loss

- Cold body and extremities

- High blood pressure

- Contracted blood vessels

- Nervous and cold perspiration

This type of UDIN causes the body to go into a flight-or-fight response; our body turns into a machine designed to solve the problem we've just encountered. This is an activation of the 'sympathetic nervous system' and is commonly experienced as a feeling of stress. Also, we know from the previous chapter that the brain, designated organ, heart, behavioral, and environmental issues change as the person tries to solve the underlying problem.

    Obsessive thinking is really interesting because this, in my opinion, explains how stress affects us mentally. It also explains the erratic behavior that we see in people whom we would normally consider rational.

To explain this, imagine that a partner (say, a male) has just walked out on you with no explanation whatsoever. This is someone you love dearly and you had no inclination that there was anything wrong. What would you be thinking? What would be going through your mind? You would be going crazy, asking yourself, 'Why did he leave?' 'What did I do wrong?' 'Is he seeing someone else?'

You might then imagine him in bed with that someone else, which would send your head into a spin. You would be obsessed with trying to find out why this had happened. Your work would suffer. You wouldn't eat or sleep. Your feet and hands would become cold as the blood in your system was directed to the muscles so that you had the energy to solve the issue – a throwback to early humans having to contend with an attack from a predator – the fight-or-flight response. Generally you wouldn't feel any pain or discomfort because your body would be operating at a heightened emergency level.

What is not obvious is that specific organs change in order to support you through this process in alignment with their function. So the breast reacts with regard to nurturing, the gut to digestion, the skin to separation, and the muscles to strength. Generally, the biological reason for all diseases is so that you are better equipped to deal with the fight-or-flight situation if the event occurs again.

We are not programmed to live in this stressed way forever. After the stressful event, at some point we may find a solution to the problem. When we do, the body reacts by repairing and rebuilding the organ that was affected. We then switch from the 'sympathetic' nervous system to the 'parasympathetic' nervous system.

Parasympathetic nervous system

This system is the antithesis of the sympathetic nervous system. While we are in this half – the Repair and Rebuild Stages – we generally feel very tired, and if there is no pain, we mostly feel very relaxed. The classic symptoms of a parasympathetic nervous system appear as:

- Fatigue and tiredness
- Good appetite
- Weight gain
- Warm body and extremities
- Low blood pressure
- Slow heart rate
- Wide blood vessels
- Perspiration, hot skin and body
- Fever

If almost all diseases are due to a stressful event, which we know is supported by scientific data, then at some point after the stress we may solve the shocking issue that made us stressed in the first place. I say 'may' because sometimes we never solve the stressful event and the body stays in a state of continuous stress.

The two systems of disease

In all my work, I've found that these two systems play a part in every disease – the stressful first half, followed by the rest-and-repair half. Biologists and the medical profession acknowledge there are two different systems, the sympathetic nervous system and the parasympathetic nervous system, but they haven't made a connection between the two.

The sympathetic and the parasympathetic nervous systems are commonly called the 'autonomic nervous system' (meaning 'not controlled by the mind'). You can see from the table below that these systems work in balance with each other and directly or indirectly affect almost every structure in the body.

Organ	Sympathetic nervous system	Parasympathetic nervous system
Heart	Rate and force increased	Rate and force decreased
Lungs	Bronchial muscle relaxed	Bronchial muscle contracted
Eyes (iris)	Dilation	Constriction
Intestines	Motility reduces	Motility, digestion, and secretions increase
Bladder	Wall muscle relaxes, sphincter closes	Wall muscle contracts, sphincter relaxes
Kidneys	Decreased urine secretion	Increased urine secretion

We actually experience these different systems constantly. However, our bodies are mostly in a sympathetic state during the day, and then at night we enter the parasympathetic state. After a shocking and stressful event, however, the body stays in the sympathetic state until a solution is found to the issue. The body then goes into the parasympathetic state.

At night, if we've experienced a shock earlier in the day and are in the sympathetic state, we may find that we can't sleep well; we'll toss and turn and sleep lightly. In a worst-case scenario, a person will experience insomnia.

Many people experience this at some time in their lives. Perhaps the night before an important job interview or exam. A sleepless night is not unusual in these situations. Following the reversal of the stressful situation, finding out whether or not you got the job, or passed or failed that exam, either meant the stress carried on until you did get what you wanted, or you gave up, or everything worked out fine for you. Once the stress has been resolved (UDIN Reversal), you would find that you needed to rest, and many people often get colds or have a bout of mild diarrhea. They feel hot and sweaty and out of sorts. The same thing happens if you stress your body to the limit. For example, running a marathon leaves you feeling exhausted, and afterward you need to rest.

These two systems are normal and well recognized in medical literature. However, what is not obvious is the long-term effect of staying in the sympathetic nervous state, the first system, due to a UDIN event. If this is a deeply intense experience and continues for a long time, it may cause failure or fatigue of an organ, such as being diagnosed with adrenal fatigue (often associated with burnout and chronic fatigue syndrome), rapid heartbeat (tachycardia), sudden weight loss (hyperthyroidism), or high blood pressure.

We all have shocks every day, and some can be UDINs, but often they are not very deep and are quickly resolved. Sometimes we are left hanging in one system, sometimes we repeat them, and in other situations we can repeat certain cycles again and again.

The six stages of disease

From an Advanced Clearing Energetics perspective, all diseases are caused by a significant emotional event (a UDIN) followed by ongoing stress (Stress Stage). If the UDIN is reversed (UDIN Reversal), the body enters the parasympathetic system: first, the body repairs itself (Repair Stage); then it faces a biological test – the 'Spike.' This point explains many of the symptoms that people experience when sick (we'll discuss the Spike in more detail in Chapter 7). Then, in the second half of the parasympathetic system, the body enters the Rebuild Stage. What seems apparent is that these six stages of disease can be used to explain the symptoms of any disease or illness. The following diagram illustrates the process:

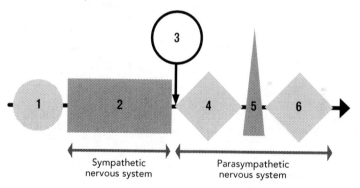

Key: the six stages of disease

1 UDIN

2 **Stress Stage:** Cold, sympathetic nervous system is running

3 **UDIN Reversal:** Unconscious or conscious process

4 **Repair Stage:** Warm, parasympathetic nervous system is running; rest and recuperation

5 **Spike:** Short, sympathetic nervous system runs; immense stress on the body; also a test for the mind, body, and heart

6 **Rebuild Stage:** Parasympathetic nervous system is running, replenishing energy reserves

Understanding the six stages

Before the disease occurs, we feel fine; we are healthy. We go through the day/night rhythm – awake during the day and asleep at night. However, let's imagine that we've been very busy at work, pushing ourselves, sleeping less and working hard, eating fast foods, drinking lots of coffee, drinking excessive amounts of alcohol, and not exercising, which means our vitality and reserves can become depleted. It's important to note, however, that we can be totally healthy for a UDIN to affect us, but usually these events occur when our vitality or life-force energy is reduced. So let's go through the six stages:

1. UDIN

We experience a UDIN that completely catches us off guard. This is the Unexpected, Dramatic, Isolating shock where we have No Strategy for dealing with the issue. During this time the brain records everything: what we see, hear, feel, taste, smell, and certain words are logged and stored. One of these senses has the most energy attached to it. Usually this is either the tone of a person's voice, or the look a person gives, or something else visual, such as a piece of jewelry. A sharp, focused sphere, seen as a ring on a CT scan, appears in the brain at a specific location, corresponding to the organ that has been picked to deal with the issue most effectively. This sphere has all the trapped energy that corresponds to the shock, which is also sending out a wave of energy, via the heart, through the whole body and externally through electromagnetic waves. This, in turn, affects our thinking, any emotion gets stored in the gut, the way in which we react socially alters, and where we are in our world, our environment, changes significantly.

2. Stress Stage

Cold, sympathetic nervous system is running.

Here we experience the second stage, which we commonly experience as stress. Our hands and feet are cold; we eat little (and the little we do eat is usually fast food, has a high sugar content, or is very acidic, e.g., processed foods). We might eat sugary carbohydrates, take recreational drugs, or drink excessively during this time because we're trying to get away from the stress we feel. We skip meals, our blood pressure increases, and we may have nervous and cold perspiration. Obsessive thinking takes over our whole lives. If this stressful stage carries on for any length of time, we lose weight. The blood is directed from the digestive tract to the muscles and vital organs, hence the reason for appetite loss.

We have a high output of glucose and an increased secretion of adrenalin, making faster reactions possible. Plus, we sleep erratically and for short periods of time. Insomnia is common. The organ that is affected changes itself either by necrosis (cell removal), as in the widening of a tube such as a blood vessel or bronchial tube, allowing more fluid/air to travel through it. Or the body builds more cells; as an example, more intestine cells are produced to aid digestion of the issue, or more gland cells are made to produce more milk to nurture a child back to health.

Depending on the type of organ and its arrangement in our body, there will be a growth of fungi, bacteria, or a virus that will go unnoticed because it is in the blood. The microbes are dormant, and the number of microbe cells produced is in direct proportion to the number of cells lost or grown. That means for every cell grown there is an equal number of cells of bacteria grown in the blood, but *only* if you are exposed to, or have the bacteria in your system. Viruses are produced during this time in a measured amount in accordance with the cell reduction. Sometimes we don't have the required fungi, bacteria, or virus in our system. If that is the case, then the body will either find it from outside in the environment or it won't be produced.

Sometimes parasites collect in the body. These seem to be excellent at removing heavy metals, e.g., mercury, from the system, and the body also determines the number of parasites. In the Stress Stage, the parasite is multiplying, getting ready for the next stage.[1] Parasites thrive in acidic environments, and in the Stress Stage the body is acidic.

Typical symptoms of the Stress Stage might be constipation, loss of strength in certain muscles, excessive energy, being able to breathe to the bottom of your lungs effortlessly with little or no mucus, flaking of the skin, increase in nasal senses, sensitivity to touch (as in breast glands), and thickening of the lower layer of the skin (dermis).

3. UDIN Reversal

Unconscious or conscious process.

The UDIN shock is resolved; either we are consciously aware of this happening or completely unconscious that something has been solved. Good examples of consciously being aware would be when we leave a very stressful relationship for good, or an argument gets completely resolved. Unconscious examples would be a reversal happening while we sleep. You wake up with a cold, having gone to bed feeling fine. Or something triggers an association, which unconsciously reminds you of a person. The reversal of the conflict happens in the same sense that triggered it. But it is opposite to the trigger, therefore a different tone that resolves the issue or an opposite picture – e.g., a person looks at you with a genuine smile instead of the angry grimace that was in the original shock. At this point the symptoms start to appear, and we will begin to experience the feeling of the Repair Stage. An example would be when you feel like the weight of the world has been lifted off your shoulders.

4. Repair Stage

Warm, parasympathetic nervous system is running; rest and recuperation.

This stage starts just after the UDIN Reversal, and then the symptoms start to feel unpleasant. You feel the relief immediately in the UDIN Reversal but, depending on the background stress, the painful symptoms may not appear until later on that day – e.g., you may have been in a meeting where you resolve something major, you get the first symptoms of a nasal cold, such as a runny nose, and you feel tired so you stress yourself a little by drinking some coffee. You have to go for a meal that night, but the symptoms get even more intense. You get a sore throat, so you take a cold remedy, which probably contains caffeine and stresses your body a little more to fight off the symptoms. You wake up the next morning with the cold.

During this time, the organ that was under stress goes into repair. If there had been a cell reduction, as in the widening of a blood vessel to allow more blood to flow, then this needs to be repaired. The cells that were taken away in the Stress Stage are replaced. In blood vessels, this results in swelling and a restriction of the blood flow. In muscles, the muscle is repaired and swells up. This is carried out by the body working in homeostasis with the fungi, bacteria, or viruses that were being produced in the blood during the Stress Stage.

In organs where there was an increase in cells (such as in the bowel or the breast glands), the extra cells are no longer required so they are eaten away by fungi or bacteria. If the bacteria are not in the system, then the issue becomes encapsulated; a thin film of skin forms around the extra cells where they lie dormant. In the gut, the parasites start to die off, as they dislike this alkaline environment. Their job has been done.

Extra water is used to support this process, hence swelling is normal where the organ needs to be repaired. The swelling is why we feel pain during this time; however, excessive swelling is due to kidney collecting tubule syndrome (see page 100). The body directs all the blood toward the digestive organs – we have warm hands and feet. Blood pressure is low, our temperature is higher than normal, and we usually have a fever. We perspire and feel hot. We feel tired and fatigued, our digestive organs receive more blood, and our appetite slowly comes back (but not in the same way as in the Rebuild Stage). Note: antifungals, antibiotics, and antivirals destroy the natural balance of the body – the fungi, bacteria, and viruses (the microbes). However, it is important to understand that in severe cases these medical interventions do save lives.

5. Spike

Short sympathetic nervous system runs; immense stress on the body; also a test for the mind, body, and heart.

The Spike is one of the most important points in the disease process, so much so that I have dedicated Chapter 7 to this phenomenon. This is where most people really think the disease or issue is either reversing or getting significantly worse. The Spike appears to be a biological test, and it also serves another purpose – that of squeezing out the water used in the Repair Stage. It is a challenging time because the symptoms can be so acute and, in some instances, can be fatal – e.g., as in a cardiac arrest.

Some of the typical symptoms are feeling panicky having previously felt totally relaxed, headache (anything from a mild headache up to a migraine), muscle cramps, muscle twitching, epileptic seizures, coughing fits, sneezing fits, and intense itching. Excessive urination is also a common factor during this time. People usually notice that they have to visit the bathroom a lot, and the amount of water passed is significantly greater than the amount they have drunk during the day. The Spike happens halfway between the start of the Repair Stage and the end of the Rebuild Stage.

6. Rebuild Stage

Parasympathetic nervous system is running, replenishing energy reserves.

After the Spike, we go into the Rebuild Stage. During this time we will still feel unwell, but the main pain has disappeared. The infections will have subsided, but we're not back to normal yet. We eat more during this period, and it is common to feel ravenously hungry. People tend to put on weight as the body rebuilds its reserves. The main repair is done. But now the body has to ensure that the organs affected are better able to deal with a possible repeat of the problem. Here we experience scarring, a Rebuild.

Our muscles increase in size, our bones are stronger at the fracture site than the surrounding unbroken bone, the skin gets thicker, or the organ generally gets stronger. As the Rebuild is being completed, further symptoms appear. The intestinal walls are rebuilt, and as that happens, our gut can feel sore and we can be sensitive to certain foods. If there was cell degradation, as in the common cold, the nasal passages, larynx, bronchi, or all three cell walls are rebuilt; we feel breathless and sneeze or spit out the excess mucus that was required to earlier repair the cell wall.

An obvious example of this is the excessive skin growth that happens when we cut ourselves. A scab appears excessive to the repair/rebuild, which is happening underneath. When the scab drops off, a scar is left. This is the same for the bronchi mucosa, and this is what we notice as we blow our nose or cough up phlegm. You will see it as yellow, brown, or slightly bloody phlegm. Plus, if you were to look at the bronchi, you would see scarring.

At the end of the Rebuild Stage, we complete the process; we start to feel better and our energy returns. This can take time; the deeper the Stress Stage, the longer this process will take. During this time there may be some remnants of the process: e.g., a scab may take a few more days before it's ready to fall off or there may still be some phlegm stuck in the bronchi or nasal passages, which we eventually cough up or end up blowing out through the nose. The intestine stops being so sensitive to certain foods. Specific organ swelling decreases and size returns to normality. Any pain subsides and eventually stops.

Eventually we feel normal and all remnants of the Rebuild Stage and any symptoms disappear, except for maybe a scar, encapsulated growths (a thin film of skin is built around the growth) or loose ends of old tissue, which are doing nothing. Generally we feel good inside and normal bodily functions are resumed. The area that was affected usually has no excessive extra biological material around it. There may be some scarring (which tends to be stronger but less durable than the original tissue). Sometimes the repair/rebuild leaves an excessive amount of skin, bone, or material that can be removed, as in a tumor that has been encapsulated, or calcification around a bone. Or there is cell reduction, such as in a dimple with acne scarring. At this time we end up feeling good, and normal day/night rhythm is resumed.

Timing of the six stages

Something really fascinating and worth noting about the six stages is that the length of time for the Stress Stage is often, but not always, equal to the length of the Repair, Spike, and Rebuild Stages put together. And the Spike often happens right in the middle, time-wise. This can mean that a practitioner trained to a high level in Advanced Clearing Energetics with enough information is able to work out exactly when the start of the disease process occurred based on when a certain stage started. I do this regularly with my clients. If I know when a client started experiencing painful symptoms, the Repair Stage, and if I can determine the timing of the Spike, then I can determine the exact time the UDIN occurred. And I'm able to tell clients exactly what time they will start to feel better. In other instances, I am able to prepare them so they can go through the Spike without fear, and in the knowledge that the body is doing what it is designed to do – heal itself.

Bacteria in the system

If we don't have the necessary bacteria in our system, possibly due to taking antibiotics, then the body will take the bacteria that it needs from its surroundings to complete the Repair Stage. This is where we need to be careful if we're on vacation or overseas. Usually we rush around like idiots getting everything prepared before we leave. We put ourselves under pressure; arguments are common (especially between partners or spouses). Our boss asks us to complete a complex project in two days (something that would normally take a week), and we have no choice but to work really hard and late. We are frustrated and angry. Other things happen that take up our precious time, making the situation worse. Most likely we experience a UDIN or two. This is a Stress Stage. Finally, we get to our destination and relax. At that time we go into the UDIN Reversal. We make up with our partners. We forget about our boss and that project. All the anger and frustration is forgotten.

The problem arises due to the fact that most of us live in such a sterile environment these days – due to antibacterial soaps, cleaners, daily bathing, etc. – or have taken antibiotics or eaten food that contains antibiotics, we often don't have the necessary bacteria in our gut to heal ourselves. So the body uses the most appropriate bacteria it can get from the environment – usually from the local food. We then find that a few days into our vacation we end up with diarrhea (the Spike). It isn't due to the food, or the cooking process, which admittedly can be very unclean. It is because the body gets and uses whatever viruses, bacteria, fungi, or parasites it requires to complete the Repair Stage. In foreign countries these bacteria are a different strain from those we have grown up with in our normal environment, which is why the reaction can be quite violent in some instances.

So when you go to a different country, the microbes are different. The people from the local area don't get the same reaction from eating their food. A friend of mine from Egypt, Dr. Khaled Al-Damallawy, told me that in Cairo the healthiest kids are from the poorest families. They have built up a stock of microbes from playing in the streets and, even though they can't afford to have antibiotics or vaccinations, they don't have anywhere near the same health issues as children from wealthier families. Many people in Egypt are confused by this social paradox, but after Dr. Khaled Al-Damallawy heard about the six stages and how microbes work in homeostasis with the body and the environment, he said it made more sense than other hypotheses.

Going back to the six stages and how people react in most cases, a healthy person will experience a full disease process – a Stress Stage followed by the 'Repair and Rebuild Stages,' including a Spike in the middle. But the elegant timing of the process can be interrupted by recreational drugs, stimulants (e.g., caffeine), or taking over-the-counter medications – e.g., painkillers such as acetylsalicylic acid (aspirin), acetaminophen (paracetamol), codeine, ibuprofen, or anti-inflammatories – because they can stimulate the system and elongate the disease process.

Swelling: Kidney collecting tubule syndrome

Excessive swelling during the healing phase is due to kidney collecting tubule syndrome. This is a separate conflict and relates specifically to the part of the kidneys that regulates water throughout the body. The UDIN that causes this to occur is an issue of feeling completely abandoned or a feeling of total isolation. Another consequence of this is feeling 'I am not going to make it.' Terminally ill patients and the elderly (particularly when placed in convalescent homes) often experience this UDIN, as they feel they are literally waiting to die.

The reason the body retains water in these areas is to prevent the body from dying of dehydration. This syndrome dates back millions of years, when humans required a survival system for being left in extremely hot or cold environments without any form of shelter.

This UDIN event causes intense water retention in and around the organ that is going through the Repair or Rebuild Stage. People experiencing this syndrome can get a swelling in the abdomen after drinking alcohol heavily, or around the legs and ankles after doing some form of sport. But it can occur in any part of the body that is going through the Repair or Rebuild Stages. The problem can repeat itself over and over again, as with chronic diseases. Examples of this are arthritis or gaining weight without eating excessively (I have known people who have put on several pounds, literally overnight, without eating anything extra).

Leukemia is another extreme example of this syndrome, being the Repair/Rebuild Stages of a bone marrow healing with this kidney collecting tubule syndrome. Other examples are swollen joints or even whole limbs. I worked with a client whose knee was the size of a small melon; the pain was so bad he was talking to his surgeon about having his leg amputated above the knee.

CROUP – FEARFULNESS

My son gets croup (laryngotracheobronchitis), a respiratory condition usually triggered by an acute viral infection of the upper airway, and it affects many young children. The medical profession doesn't know what causes it, but from an Advanced Clearing Energetics perspective, the reason for it is simple and can easily be explained and treated.

My son has a UDIN perhaps from school, typically a fear that someone is going to hit him or take away something that he owns, such as a toy he loves. He lives in the Stress Stage until the UDIN Reversal. This affects his upper bronchial tract, but there are no noticeable physical symptoms, although behaviorally and environmentally he becomes manic, doesn't go to bed at his normal time, doesn't eat well, has a lot of excess energy, and doesn't want to go to school – the Stress Stage.

When the UDIN is reversed he gets a bronchial cold, except he also gets kidney collecting tubule syndrome. His lungs fill with extra water, which doesn't cause any problem while he is awake, but as soon as he lies down to go to sleep, the water slowly trickles down into his throat causing the horrendous croup cough. There is little or nothing your medical doctor can do except give steroids to reverse the symptoms and push the body back into the Stress Stage.

Sometimes antibiotics are prescribed to suppress the bronchial cold. They can take days to kick in and often will do nothing because this is a viral infection, not a bacterial one.

The answer is very simple; during this time I sit Oliver up in his bed, supporting him with pillows. He then sleeps, doesn't cough, and gets well very quickly. He is now getting to the age where I can probably work with him to clear the UDIN, although it only occurred once last year. He's four as of 2013.

I was originally taught that kidney collecting tubule syndrome was impossible to reverse, and for many years I tried and failed to solve this problem for clients. However, my landmark event was with a lady in Denmark whose arm had tripled in size. She was in so much pain and her intense screaming was keeping people awake in the five-story terraced apartment building where she lived. I worked with her overnight for 18 hours, and the swelling went down and her arm returned to normal.

Later on I had the same success with other people with limbs that had swollen, but it took a long time to find the UDIN. One such person was Susie Shelmerdine, an EFT and Matrix Reimprinting trainer who had a swelling in her upper gums that lasted over two months; she could not speak during this time, as the swelling affected her that much. While I was working with her, she resolved the UDIN moment (UDIN Reversal), and the swelling subsided overnight.

After I developed Advanced Clearing Energetics, I was able to find the UDIN in minutes instead of many hours, which has transformed this syndrome from something life-threatening and extremely painful into something easily manageable.

Dr. Diana Stephanie-Hunyady, a medical doctor and one of my master students of Advanced Clearing Energetics, said, upon hearing about this syndrome: 'Kidney collecting tubule syndrome accounts for over 50 percent of all the diseases a doctors sees in their practice,' and she agreed that this was probably the reason for the symptoms seeming 100 percent worse than they really are.

Doctors try and alleviate this problem by giving diuretics, but they don't seem to work that well on kidney collecting tubule syndrome; they do stop further increases in swelling, but they don't decrease the swelling. Steroids, which are often used in these issues, can actually make the problem worse as they exacerbate the kidneys' energetic reason for producing more water, and therefore increase the water retention and swelling.

Natural healing

If you're unwell, it is always best to seek a medical diagnosis, but then, if possible, allow the body to go through the six stages of healing without drugs, as this usually works for most healthy people. On the whole, people experience pain and illness in the Repair and Rebuild Stages. Drugs and other therapies are likely to slow down the healing process and can hinder the person from getting well, and we do need to complete the disease process at some time.

I'm not against drugs, and there are times when the effects of these drugs are useful, as in the case of one of my clients with multiple brain tumors. She took a small dose of steroids and was able to function, having been bedridden for a month and unable to move her head because every time she did she would end up with a massive headache. I believe that most brain tumors are due to a ring in the brain healing along with kidney collecting tubule syndrome; the tumor literally collects excessive water in and around the brain relay, which is in its Repair or Rebuild Stage.

A small dosage of acetylsalicylic acid (aspirin) is often prescribed for people who have experienced heart problems. This keeps them in a minor Stress Stage. For example, my father-in-law takes a small dose of aspirin daily; he had triple bypass surgery in 1999. He is constantly mildly stressed and also slightly anxious about everything. This is a good thing, because if he went into Repair Stage he could suffer a cardiac arrest in the Spike again which, at his age of 70-plus years, would be very worrying for him. Therefore, it is better to have a little bit of stress than to solve the problem completely, and he seems happy to live with this level of mild anxiety.

Many of us live in a stressful environment in the West, and just drinking large amounts of tea and coffee every day stresses our bodies. At one time I removed all food-related stimulants from my life: tea, coffee, sugar, and processed foods, in order to experience what it was like to live a food-induced stress-free lifestyle. I also gave up red meat because when an animal is killed in a slaughterhouse, the collective fear causes a rush of adrenalin that passes through the body, because the animal is stressed. This means that if you don't eat steak very often and you have a rare piece of fillet steak, you can get a rush of energy from the meat as your body digests the adrenalin that was in the blood of the slaughtered animal.[2]

The experience of living without the normal food-induced stress was so enjoyable that I've tried to maintain my diet in that way. I also got down to my optimum weight very quickly. However, in reality, traveling and staying with many friends around the world makes it challenging to always stick to this diet.

The fact is that we are healing machines; we go in and out of these stages every day in some form or fashion, and the body is easily capable of adapting to and dealing with these problems. We are designed to do it. It's only when the shocks are so deep and intense – as in a UDIN shock – that there is a problem, or the shocks repeat themselves as with chronic illnesses or with cancers, which are often due to a decision that the person cannot survive the UDIN.

Just to illustrate this point, I was delivering a training seminar in Bristol, UK, and happened to be talking about the six stages. In the back of the room one of my assistants was typing on his computer, which really annoyed one of the delegates, John, and he developed a tinnitus (the Stress Stage of a hearing conflict). The tinnitus was at exactly the same frequency as the tapping of the keys. This is what happens with tinnitus; the frequency matches the tone that the person doesn't want to hear. After 30 minutes of this annoying typing, John spoke to the assistant and asked him politely to stop typing. He apologized and stopped. John then experienced a minor loss of hearing for 30 minutes, with a small thumping in his eardrums for one minute halfway (at about 15 minutes), as he went through the Spike. After this time the issue completely cleared up.

The majority of aches and pains in situations like this go unnoticed, but I have found that these six stages seem to work so elegantly that, although there are as yet no research papers that confirm the process of the six stages, the empirical evidence is undeniable. Remember, the six stages involve the sympathetic nervous system followed by the parasympathetic nervous system. Both these systems are completely understood by the medical profession, but they haven't joined the two. Time and time again, the six stages allow me and other people I've trained in Advanced Clearing Energetics to establish exactly the root cause of a disease process by working back from the specific changes a client has gone through.

Evidence for the six stages of disease

There is some evidence pointing to the link between the Stress, Repair, Spike, and Rebuild Stages in Bruce Lipton's groundbreaking book *The Biology of Belief*.[3] The body has 50 trillion cells working and repairing, and it was thought that this process happened simultaneously. However, Lipton found that this was not the case:

> *'The mechanisms that support growth and protection cannot operate simultaneously. Cells cannot simultaneously move backwards and forwards.'*[4]

This theory fits with the accepted two different systems – sympathetic and parasympathetic – that, like the cells, operate at different times.

Similarly, a 2005 research paper[5] examining the work of Geerd Hamer, and referencing the earlier theories of Aaron Antonovsky, Abraham Harold Maslow, and Viktor Emil Frankl points to the six stages being true.

Dr. George Kulik, an assistant professor of cancer biology and senior researcher, wrote in an article in the US publication *Science Daily*:

> 'Scientists from Wake Forest University School of Medicine are the first to report that the stress hormone epinephrine causes changes in prostate and breast cancer cells which may make them resistant to cell death. These data imply that emotional stress may contribute to the development of cancer and may also reduce the effectiveness of cancer treatments.'[6]

Certain cells grow in the Stress Stage, such as prostate cancer cells and glandular breast cancer cells, hence the ineffectiveness of many cancer treatments to shrink a tumor because traditional cancer treatments such as chemotherapy and radiotherapy put the body under immense stress.

It is also interesting that scientists look at cells in petri dishes, but omit to consider that stress is linked to disease (most probably after a UDIN shock). Scientists don't talk to the people whose cells are being worked on. They know the mind and body are linked but fail to include this vital fact when studying a group of cells. A fundamental flaw in all medical scientific research is that 'the mind' is not there to influence the cells. In *The Intention Experiment*, Lynne McTaggart explains in great detail how the phenomenon of the mind influences everything, including the cells in our body.

The medical profession doesn't know why a cancer grows. They have no idea that some cancers grow after a stressful event has occurred (e.g., bowel and glandular breast cancer), and usually only really show as lumps one to three years later. Some grow in the Repair and Rebuild

Stages, such as leukemia, which is the Repair Stage of the bones (along with kidney collecting tubule syndrome) – the Stress Stage is osteoporosis, therefore cell degradation. In the liver, which has ducts leading into the gall bladder, the Stress Stage is cirrhosis; the Repair Stage is hepatoma or hepacellular carcinoma. Interesting recent discoveries suggest that the virus thought to cause this cancer is the hepatitis A, B, C, D, E, and G virus. (The missing hepatitis F virus is a hypothetical virus linked to hepatitis. There have been several candidates for the hepatitis F virus since 1990, but none have been substantiated.) The medical profession tries to kill the virus but hasn't thought about why the virus appears at this time, in the Repair Stage.

Metastasis – secondary cancers

As regards the feared metastasis, or secondary cancers, we can also attribute these to the six stages. The common notion that cancerous cells travel through the body and attach themselves to specific organs at random has never been proven. It is a hypothesis that has little or no scientific or medical grounding. This hypothesis was created because some cells show up in certain places, such as ovarian or testicular cancer cells showing up in other parts of the body, e.g., the lungs. But this happens only in 5 percent or fewer cases. The reason for this is a burst ovarian cyst, usually caused by kidney collecting tubule syndrome (see page 100), where excessive water collects in and around the organ, making it swell. The burst tissue travels through the body and attaches itself to other organs, which give it a blood supply, and it begins to grow. It is not life-threatening unless it affects a person mechanically, because it will stop growing, in the case of ovarian cysts, after nine months.

The other 95 percent of secondary cancers are made from the same cells in the organ itself. The cells of a primary cancer such as breast cancer do not show up in the lungs as a secondary cancer. Those secondary cells are made of lung cells.

What is causing these secondary cancers? A medical diagnosis of such magnitude as cancer. Imagine that a woman is told she has breast cancer and then is told she has to have the breast removed. Understandably, this can cause a multitude of UDIN moments, and depending on how the woman reacts, could cause any one of a number of secondary cancers, such as:

- Fear of death – lung cancer

- Fear of being unable to provide for the family – liver cancer

- A severe lack of self-worth and failure – bone cancer (especially in the back)

- Personal crisis (femininity under threat) – lymph cancer

All of these cancers don't come from the original cells in the breast but from separate UDIN shocks.

As we delve deeper into the six stages, I'm certain that you will find, as I have and as has everyone I've taught and worked with, that these six stages are undeniable. Every disease, from a simple pimple on the face to a life-threatening cancer, has its origin and explanation for growth and healing in the six stages. Even with every spontaneous remission, a person goes through these six stages. During these so-called miracles, the person goes through a really hot, sweaty time where they almost die, only to come out the other side healed: the Spike (see also page 128).

In the next chapter we'll look at why certain symptoms appear and disappear, and then reappear, why people can be ill for ten years with chronic fatigue or with eczema, or suffer their entire adult lives with IBS or acne. Why people with multiple sclerosis have attacks, and why Parkinson's patients don't shake at night but do shake all day. We'll also take a look at allergies: why they suddenly start and what really triggers them.

CHAPTER 6

WHY DISEASES KEEP RECURRING

'The immune system didn't evolve for allergy.
Why in a hundred billion years of evolution
would we evolve a response for allergy?'

Dr. Joel Weinstock, American author and gastroenterologist

So what causes allergies, chronic diseases, recurring issues, and cancers to regrow? Why do they do it? Do dust mites cause asthma? Why doesn't steroid cream cure eczema? Is laundry detergent responsible for skin rashes? Is IBS caused just by food, and why do certain foods cause it to be worse while others are okay? Why doesn't anyone, medical, complementary, or alternative, know how to cure these problems? They promise the world, but often they never fully deliver.

According to Advanced Clearing Energetics, there are six stages of a disease process, but there are people who seemingly have ongoing diseases. Do these people then go through the six stages? If they do, then how does that happen?

To explain this we need to briefly visit the start of a disease again. We talked comprehensively about this event, the UDIN (see page 55). You may remember the special criteria that cause a conflict shock to get trapped in our neurological system; and how, during this time, our brain, organs, heart, and behavioral and environmental situations all change to support us through the disease process.

When a UDIN happens, all the information that was going on at that time gets trapped. The neurology seems to take each sense – e.g., the tone/sound of the voice of a person, the tone/sound of an object, the look on the face, pictures of specific things, any external touch, any specific smell or taste (including any food that may be eaten at that time) – and it holds this event so it can deal with it and resolve it at a later date.

We learn by association, and this event is the same; two things get linked, such as when you hear that special tune reminding you of that incredible moment. When you see a foreign word, it is not until someone explains what it means that you learn.

The same is happening here in the UDIN. However, the event is so challenging that the body takes the event and holds it in the neurology. We can see this trapped energy in the brain and organs under a CT scan. It shows up in a brain CT scan as a ring, in a location that corresponds embryonically to the organ that is affected; the organ will also have one of these rings on it. Visit www.whyamisick.com to see some examples.

Trapped energy

According to Professor Peter Fraser, this trapped energy vibrates as a standing wave, at the same rate as the waves (x-rays) used in CT scanning. This also makes sense as regards quantum mechanics and the work of Milo Wolfe, concerning the way in which energy causes atoms to move and work together to create patterns. More about this in my next book, *How Can I Heal?*

However, we know that these rings are actually balls of trapped energy. You can see this under specific types of CT scan slicing, where it is possible to make out that the energy is not a two-dimensional ring but a three-dimensional ball. It is also worth noting that these balls of energy are not static; they change over time. The brain is not a static organ, as portrayed in a CT scan, but changes from moment to moment.

The trapped energy and information in this ball holds the key to why a disease becomes chronic, or why an allergy to a specific substance appears. The energy ball seems to hold information in it. This information acts as a warning mechanism to prevent us from repeating the same mistake. This type of early warning system and holding on to information can be demonstrated by people suffering from post-traumatic stress disorder, such as soldiers who have seen battle, fire fighters, paramedics, and nurses.[1]

Psychiatrist Dr. Don Condie and neurobiologist Dr. Guochuan Tsai used an fMRI scanner to study the brain patterns of a woman with a multiple personality disorder. In this disorder, the woman switched regularly between her normal personality and an alter ego called 'Guardian.' The two personalities had separate memory systems and quite different strategies. The fMRI[2] brain scan showed that each of these two personalities used different neural networks (different areas of the brain lit up when each personality emerged).

As the following example illustrates, trapped energy can change everything in our lives.

ECZEMA – SEPARATION ISSUES

Katrina came up on stage during one of my training sessions in 2007. From the age of 11 she'd suffered from eczema, and it covered her whole body from time to time. Her doctor had prescribed steroid creams; and she'd tried every medical, complementary, and alternative solution, too, as well as working with a nutritionist. Consequently, the eczema only affected her right inner arms, around the elbow joint, and a few other areas here and there.

Several of the delegates and I inspected the eczema; and it was red, hot, and according to Katrina, itchy. Katrina described how sometimes the skin would crack and ooze, and it would become very painful to the touch, as it appeared at the moment.

Katrina was studying with me and knew the eczema was due to a separation conflict, and she had some idea that it had to do with being separated from her family in New Zealand. However, she couldn't understand why it didn't disappear completely or what kept triggering it.

I asked her to clap her hands and established that she was right-wired (see page 116 for more on 'wiring'), and so felt separated from her father. In response, Katrina told us that she missed her father but didn't feel separated from him because they kept in regular contact.

Now I know that what triggers disease can be totally beyond conscious awareness. So I probed and asked her to run the last conversation she'd had with her father through her mind again, and whether there was a point where she felt separated or disconnected from him in some way.

She stopped, looked away, ran the conversation through her mind, and at one point went bright red. I said, 'Stop there. What was he saying then?' She looked at me in amazement, and replied, 'He was talking about me and that I have always wanted to work with food, career-wise, and he has always disapproved of me doing the food stuff.'

Simply by isolating the trigger, Katrina reported that her eczema no longer felt itchy, lost its redness, and felt cooler. Other delegates confirmed that her skin had changed dramatically in the space of a few minutes. They touched her palms and they were cold. The skin where the eczema had been was also cold to the touch, the redness had disappeared, the oozing had stopped, and Katrina said, 'It feels desensitized, as if it is not my skin.'

A month later I saw Katrina again, and she explained that after the training the eczema had disappeared, and she really understood why it had been there. However, she had a lot of eczema around both sides of her face and hands, and I asked her what the reason was for this problem now.

She told me that she had always had a dream of owning her own specialized food restaurant, one that produced healing food made in a unique way – some of it raw, some of it specially cooked. As she spoke, her eyes lit up. She said that she wanted to combine her training with nutritional healing.

Her father had always criticized her obsession with cooking and her lack of ambition, and she had compromised her life to this belief, and felt not only separated from her father but, more important, from herself. This explained why the eczema was showing up on both hands and both sides of her face at this time. Her inner and outer worlds were being affected.

Here's what Katrina said when she wrote to me in 2009: 'Before my healing with Richard I used to "hate" my eczema. But over the two years I have learned to be thankful whenever my eczema gets triggered. It guides me to keep doing what I love. Even today, if I let fearful thoughts enter my mind about not being able to do what I want with my life, my eczema can flare up. Fortunately, nowadays, thanks to Richard and the healing modalities I learned from him, I'm always able to understand why it is happening and as such can quickly change my state so today the eczema rarely happens.'

Wiring

How we are wired relates to which side of our body will react to certain issues. If an issue shows up on the same hand that is the leading hand, then the problem has to do with outside issues in our world, such as conflicts with our business, boss, friends, or father.

If the issue shows up on the opposite side (non-leading hand) of the body, then it has to do with the inner world: mother, children, or anything we consider as a child, such as a business that is our 'baby' or pet.

There is some proof about being left- or right-wired in identical twins; one will be left-wired and the other right-wired. Nature has a way of ensuring we react differently to different shocks. There is also plenty of empirical evidence (such as with Katrina, above) indicating that the hand-clapping and the content relating to a father or mother issue seems time and time again to bring up the cause of the disease.

There is also research that concludes that the two brain hemispheres have different functions. Some say it is pseudoscience, others not. I think it is not that great a leap to conclude that there might be a link to how we react as humans to specific conflicts. You can also visit www.whyamisick.com to see a video of how to check for wiring.

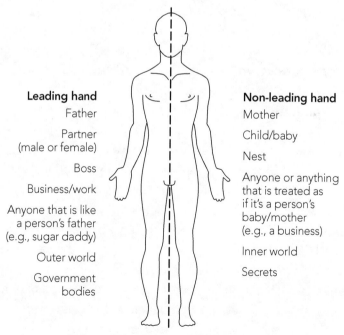

Leading hand
Father

Partner
(male or female)

Boss

Business/work

Anyone that is like
a person's father
(e.g., sugar daddy)

Outer world

Government
bodies

Non-leading hand
Mother

Child/baby

Nest

Anyone or anything
that is treated as
if it's a person's
baby/mother
(e.g., a business)

Inner world

Secrets

Left- vs right-wiring in the human body

How a UDIN causes disease

The reason that the emotions, pictures, or tones of voices of the UDIN shock become trapped is thought to be a warning signal. As discussed earlier, during the UDIN, all the pictures, sounds, feelings, tastes, smells, and words are recorded and then stored, and this shows up as an emotional ball in the brain that corresponds to the location in the body. This emotional ball is similar to a 'part,' which is a term used in NLP, hypnotherapy, and cognitive behavioral therapy (CBT) – a mainstream psychological treatment in the UK and in many other parts of the world for dealing with mental health issues such as anxiety and depression.

The theory about parts is well understood and based on the fact that when a trauma occurs, a part of the unconscious mind becomes separated from the rest of the nervous system. The reason for this is so that the person can carry on surviving without having to deal with the traumatic event. However, the unconscious mind knows that this event will need to be resolved at some time. When it thinks it is appropriate, it will bring up the emotion for re-evaluation by the conscious mind. This normally happens just before we are about to go to sleep, or when we are feeling relaxed.

You've probably experienced this yourself in some manner. Just think about the delayed shock you or other people you know have experienced after a traumatic experience. The basis behind the theory of the unconscious mind separating from the whole comes from the teachings of my friend and Master NLP trainer Dr. Tad James. The notion of parts comes from Gestalt therapy, which has many of its foundations in Freudian psychoanalysis and was developed by Fritz Perls, a German psychologist and psychotherapist.

'Parts' are similar to trapped emotions or beliefs, but unlike these states of mind, they are completely separate from the rest of the unconscious mind and have their own personality, set of beliefs, and values about life. Also, 'parts' can sometimes believe that they separately control the whole of the body and the unconscious mind.

What I've noticed by working with thousands of clients is that if people have experienced an unpleasant event in their childhood, or earlier life, where a lot of emotion was trapped or they took on a false belief, then the issue will still need to be resolved.

For example, imagine an experience where a young person goes through a trauma such as the loss of a parent, which results in a lot of trapped emotion. The emotion then needs to be resolved and a pattern is started. Even though later on in life we may consciously believe that we have dealt with the problem, it appears in our lives as a pattern that plays over and over again. We are unaware of it and unable to control the emotion. Carl Jung, founder of analytical psychology, talked about this phenomenon in his book *Psychological Types*.

This pattern then plays throughout the life of the person. The trapped emotion creates ongoing issues with relationships, such as being unnecessarily jealous or, perhaps, choosing a partner who is a mother or father figure. I've seen this behavior in many of my clients, close friends, and even myself: blatantly repeating the same pattern over and over again, such as divorcing one person because the behavior of that person became unbearable, and then remarrying someone seemingly completely different, only to find out six months into the marriage they are in the same boat as before. One of my closest friends has done this four times in his life.

We attract into our lives similar situations that we need to resolve. This then causes us to re-create the whole problem again. It is as if the unconscious mind wants us to resolve the problem and puts us back into the same situation time and time again. This, from my experience, shows up as a minor ailment or a recurring pain that often goes unnoticed. However, if an event is a UDIN, then a 'part' is created, and this 'part' will create a disease.

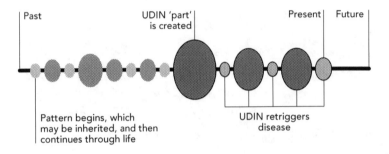

Diagram showing how a UDIN can retrigger disease

In our past, either from our parents or other influences, an unresolved UDIN sometimes starts a pattern in our own lives, which then affects our behavior and personality, causing us to relive the UDIN. Sometimes we do resolve the problem and make changes in our lives, but if we don't, then we experience the UDIN and a 'part' is created in us. That 'part' can then be re-triggered, causing a chronic disease.

Early warning system

Another interesting phenomenon about 'parts' is that there is always an underlying positive intention as to why they are there. It is as if we have a positive inbuilt early warning system, so we avoid going back to the same environment or interacting with the same person. However, if we do interact with the same environment/person, then our body already has the program for all the necessary organ and behavioral reactions to deal with the problem again.

This would explain why Katrina's eczema didn't disappear completely. A 'part' was formed, which was triggered from time to time as an early warning signal, and her comments in 2009 back that up (see page 116).

How chronic diseases occur

As shown by the diagram below, chronic disease is simply the 'part' repeating, as it is triggered again and again.

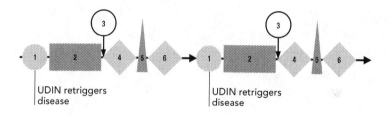

UDIN retriggers disease

UDIN retriggers disease

Key: a UDIN 'part' can retrigger and lead to chronic illness

1 UDIN: Retriggered

2 Stress Stage: Cold, sympathetic nervous system is running

3 UDIN Reversal: Unconscious or conscious process

4 Repair Stage: Warm, parasympathetic nervous system is running; rest and recuperation

5 Spike: Short sympathetic nervous system runs; immense stress on the body; also a test for the mind, body, and heart

6 Rebuild Stage: Parasympathetic nervous system is running, replenishing energy reserves

This trigger is often unconscious, as with Katrina's experience with her father always criticizing her (see page 115). Other conditions that a person might retrigger include chronic back pain, asthma, arthritis, IBS, eczema, severe acne, MS, or osteoporosis, to name but a few.

The first disease process occurs, and subsequent disease processes are retriggered by association: the same voice tone or look on a person's face, or going back to the place where the UDIN occurred.

Chronic disease in our genes

This notion also has its theory in epigenetics. A traumatic event that affected our grandparents, such as drought or starvation, can have repercussions on our offspring, and even our grandchildren. Once triggered by a new emotional event (e.g., a child screaming when it is denied certain food and being punished for screaming), this could trigger obesity or even early-onset diabetes.

This is thought to explain why some children are born with such diseases. If the event is traumatic enough, such as a mother starving herself in order to stay slim, or arguing continually with the father while pregnant, it could trigger a dormant disease, the pattern may be passed down through future generations.

Repeating the pattern similar to a grandparent's or great-grandparent's UDIN moment, the DNA of the grandchildren may express itself with the same alterations in the body, e.g., to eat excessively, in order to put on enough weight to survive an impending famine.

You may think that this cannot be true, but worldwide research into epigenetics has found plenty of supporting evidence. Most people are aware that eye color, height, and pattern of hair color are genetically inherited from their parents.[3] To change the genetic code takes 20 generations, and it was thought that DNA rules our biological makeup. However, research undertaken since 2006 has found that traumatic events such as famines, wars, and terrorist attacks (e.g., 9/11) can have a dramatic effect on how a gene is expressed.[4] Genes are not our only destiny. The environmental conditions, such as nutrition, lifestyle, inherited stress, etc., can have an effect on present and future generations.

This means that the UDIN moment can be predestined, an imprint passed down from our parents or even further back, or through other environmental circumstances. Often when I go back and clear the trapped energy from clients, it doesn't come from them but from an event perhaps in their great-great-great-grandmother's line. Someone they've never met or even knew. Once the energy is shifted, the client's issue then completes the disease process and doesn't return.

Allergies

Allergies also seem to have their origin in this theory. If you can imagine that during a traumatic event, a UDIN, everything that was going on at that time becomes linked. So tastes and smells become linked to a disease process. If you were eating an orange at the time of the UDIN, then that can trigger a disease process in the future.

An allergy can affect earlier generations and then be passed down to an individual. Or it can be due to a shock while in-utero. More likely, however, the reaction happens in childhood. Take nut allergies, for example; there will have been a conflict shock as the person was eating or swallowing nuts or a product that contained nuts, and the two became linked. The stress of a shock is linked to the nuts by association.

FOOD ALLERGY – LOSS

Kwesi discovered that he had an allergy to apples and the problem started when his father left for Ghana from Germany when Kwesi was five. His father left him and his mother to fend for themselves, and the intense realization that his father had gone for good came about as he walked to school with his mother as a young boy.

Ever since that time he was unable to eat an apple without having a minor, but discomforting, reaction. A practitioner worked with Kwesi to find the shock, and at the same time she resolved the issue by collapsing the emotion around the time when he felt the problem, using kinesiology.

Kwesi told me sometime later that the street he walked down with his mother was lined with apple trees and there would have been apples growing in abundance when his father left. He wasn't eating an apple at the time of the conflict, as far as he could remember, but he reckoned that the scent of the apples and his emotions had become symbolically linked.

After clearing the emotion, Kwesi was able to eat apples and reported no ill effects, even days later. Several months after the therapy, he reported that he still had no ill effects from eating apples and was very pleased, as it had caused him some minor issues in the past.

I've worked with many clients suffering with allergies and found the same to be true. A UDIN shock causes certain allergens, such as flower or grass pollen, fur, or dust to become linked in the same strange way. Removing the original shock stops the client from experiencing the reaction again.

HAY FEVER – INHERITANCE

One of my first therapeutic interventions was helping a young woman who suffered from hay fever. I distinctly remember that the issue wouldn't disappear until I asked her to go back to before she was conceived and clear the issue from before her birth, something we teach with Advanced Clearing Energetics.

Once she did this, pollen no longer affected her, and I had her smelling roses and flowers with no ill effects. Later that summer, she visited her family home and her mother was flabbergasted to see her during the grass-cutting season, when the pollen count was at its highest – ironically, her parents were farmers. My client nonchalantly told her mother that she had cleared out an issue from Grandmamma (UDIN), thereby making the problem disappear. Her mother said, 'But Grandmamma is dead', to which she replied, 'Not in my body she wasn't.'

In this chapter we've explored the significance of the UDIN, and how what gets stored during this time plays an important role in causing a disease to become chronic. It also explains why allergies to seemingly normal things are created. In the next chapter, we'll explore another strange phenomenon that causes challenging symptoms; why migraines happen; and what causes asthma attacks, seizures, and even fatal cardiac arrests. We will approach this in the strange world of the Spike.

CHAPTER 7

THE SPIKE

"'Healing," Papa would tell me, "is not a science, but the intuitive art of wooing nature.'"

W. H. Auden, English poet

The Spike appears to be such an innocent part of the disease process. As you look at the Spike in between the Repair and Rebuild Stages you may wonder what Mother Nature is doing by adding this stage, exactly halfway between the UDIN Reversal and the end of the Rebuild Stage.

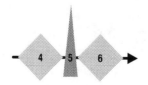

Key: the healing Spike

4 Repair Stage: Warm, parasympathetic nervous system is running; rest and recuperation

5 Spike: Short sympathetic nervous system runs; immense stress on the body; also a test for the mind, body, and heart

6 Rebuild Stage: Parasympathetic nervous system is running, replenishing energy reserves

The Repair/Rebuild Stages are incredible enough, so what is the body doing by adding this little Spike? This Spike is responsible for causing so many horrible acute symptoms, such as excruciating pain, fainting, seizures, and sometimes death. So what is this Spike and why is it there?

The Spike is thought to be a repeat of the original symptoms that initially triggered the issue. In Advanced Clearing Energetics, it is an event that has the effect of checking whether the person (or animal) is capable of being a useful member of the group or society. Do they have something to contribute that will enhance the survival or progression of their species? These are the questions that I believe are being asked during this time. This conclusion has been drawn from observations of the Spike in myself and watching animals and humans alike.

The Spike also has another purpose at a biological level. During the Repair Stage, there is a build-up of water in and around the organ and the brain relay. Once this stage has been completed, the water is no longer required. Since the body needs to eliminate the water, it squeezes it out from the organ and also out from the brain relay at the same time.

This gives rise to and explains the symptoms experienced during the Spike. In the affected organ, we experience cramping seizures of one sort or another in different organs, e.g., muscle cramps. This cramping pushes the excess water out of the body along with the debris from the repair. This can include waste products produced from the actions of the fungi, bacteria, and viruses plus anything else that is no longer required. Other less obvious symptoms are stomach cramps, which can often end in diarrhea. During these times we often feel cold, anxious, and out of sorts. Comparing this to how we felt before this stage (hot and lethargic), it would appear that the Stress Stage is repeating itself.

Most people can remember a time when they had a bout of influenza, but even if you have been lucky enough to avoid it, I'm sure you'll recognize this story.

INFLUENZA – THE SPIKE

Several years ago I had a bout of flu and was confined to my bed, exhausted and aching all over. I was boiling hot, sweating, and unable to move. I felt shattered, and all I wanted to do was sleep.

Halfway through the afternoon, I started to feel better. So much so that I got out of bed, showered, got dressed, and went back to work. An hour later I was freezing, and I felt really strange and full of excess energy. I went back to bed and wrapped myself in the bed covers, shivering with cold. My head was spinning. I felt alert but at the same time uncomfortable. A headache started to develop on the right-hand side of my head, just behind my right eye and a little in front of my ear.

Now I started to feel really worried. An hour ago I was laid up in bed with no energy; now I felt wired and had a thumping headache. Gradually my headache subsided, the shivering ceased, and my body temperature returned to normal. I also needed to urinate often, meaning more urine came out than the water I had drunk over the past few days, and I brought up a large amount of phlegm in an uncomfortable coughing fit.

After this had passed, I started to feel better and, thinking it was all over, I decided to get up and start work again. Within the hour I was back in bed, exhausted, feeling hot and out of sorts. I slept until the next day whereupon I awoke feeling much better but a little fragile. The day after that I felt fine.

If you think back to your own experiences, I'm certain that you can recall having been through one of these Spikes at some time during your life, even if it has only been diarrhea, a coughing fit, or a thumping headache. All of these are symptoms of the Spike.

What I've also observed is that the location of the headache relates to the location of the brain relay that is affected. This is because the water is being squeezed out of the relay in the brain at the same time it is being squeezed out of the organ. The brain acts like a pump, squeezing out the excess water, which has collected in the brain relay in the Repair Stage, and forcing it out through the ventricles of the brain, back into the body, where it is excreted through urine and sweat. This action can feel like a thumping action from within. There are no pain receptors inside the brain, so the thumping comes from the cramping and swelling of the brain, which pushes and pulls upon the outer skin that protects the brain.

It isn't uncommon to feel excessive pressure behind the eyes, above the forehead, around the ears, and at the back of the head near the neck. These symptoms also explain why migraine sufferers experience light spots behind the eyes before and after the pain – they could be explained by the pumping starting to occur. Migraine sufferers usually tell me that they experience these symptoms time and time again, sometimes feeling so bad that they have to shut off all light and lie down in a darkened room until the migraine passes. What is interesting is that instead of feeling tired, they feel restless.

Other well-known examples of the Spike are fainting, blacking out, epileptic seizures, asthma attacks, diarrhea, vomiting, coughing or sneezing fits, shaking or twitching of one muscle group, numbness, intense itching, panic attacks, heartburn, cardiac arrests, and coughing up or passing blood through urine.

These symptoms can last seconds, minutes, hours,or even days. They can also repeat themselves continually during the day, but disappear at night, as with Parkinson's disease.

Spontaneous remission

Anyone who experiences a spontaneous remission from a terminal illness goes through a time when symptoms follow those of the Spike. In other words, they become very ill with acute symptoms before they get better.

They report that there was a time between life and death, but that once this had passed, they knew that they were on the road to recovery. I personally thought that spontaneous remissions meant that the person woke up and the disease had miraculously disappeared. It was only after doing some research that I discovered that every one of those people who had experienced spontaneous remission went through a stage, which involved an intense Spike.[1]

Although there seems to be no direct proof of the Spike, what it can explain, however, is certain diseases such as asthma, headaches, and death (due to a cardiac arrest) while the body comes out of the Repair Stage. However, there is some clinical evidence that the Spike has been noted in homeopathy and in medical literature.

Observations of clients taking homeopathic treatments frequently reveal that when the body releases toxins, which have been stored, they are eliminated and the symptoms are temporarily reversed. This lasts for several hours or sometimes two to three days, always passing as quickly as it came on. Those clients who experience these symptoms usually continue to heal completely. There is also some homeopathic literature that states that if clients don't experience the repeat of the original symptoms, then they won't fully recover.

Homeopath Constantine Hering discovered that there are three basic principles regarding these symptoms, which fit with my observations in Advanced Clearing Energetics:

1   All cures come from the inside to the outside.

2   They come from the head down.

3   They are in reverse order, so they show up in the opposite order to which they started.

The symptoms of the Spike have also been noted in what has been recognized as the Herxheimer reaction (also known as the Jarisch-Herxheimer or Herx). Dr. Adolf Jarisch (1860–1902) and Dr. Karl Herxheimer (1861–1942) noticed that when treating syphilitic symptoms of the skin, they would often get worse before they got better. The patients would develop a fever, night sweats, and nausea and vomiting; and the skin lesions would become larger and swell before settling down and healing. These symptoms would last a few hours or two to three days before the lesions would resolve. The intensity of the reaction was reflected by the intensity of the inflammation in the first place.

The Herxheimer reaction is thought to occur when a large number of toxins are released due to the death of bacteria – often as a result of taking an antibiotic. Common symptoms are headaches, fever, and myalgia. How typical symptoms of the Spike in between the Repair and Rebuild Stages relate to excessive bacteria and the relationship between antibiotics can be explained with the six stages. The Herxheimer reaction is probably the Spike, although the hypothesis that this is due to the release of toxins is based on observations and not clinical trials.[2]

Related research seems to confirm that the Spike is linked to massive electrical changes in certain organs. Examples of this are the changes of electrical impulses in the brain that occur during an epileptic seizure. In my opinion, this further confirms the brain–organ link in Advanced Clearing Energetics and the Spike.

When someone has an epileptic seizure, there is a high amount of electrical activity, which can be measured using an EEG (electroencephalography) machine. There are also convulsions and violent shaking of the body, which occur suddenly and then disappear, and fit the symptoms of the Spike. These epileptic seizures can be life-threatening and can lead to a stroke. After a seizure, a person can lose the ability to speak, other bodily functions are severely impaired, limbs become temporarily paralyzed, and involuntary passing of water is common. In my experience and in most cases when these symptoms have passed, the person quickly returns to normal, which can take anything from a few hours to several days.[3]

Many of my cancer clients have told me that they have had an epileptic seizure. Some have had severe reactions from it, while others go through the cycle and fully recover. Others have no energy left in their bodies to complete the process and, unfortunately, die from lack of vitality and not from the cancer (all of these clients have had chemotherapy and/or radiotherapy). This is what I mean by the body testing to determine if the person is capable of being useful in the group and can contribute to society. Maybe 'Mother Nature' is questioning: 'Will the person assist the tribe in its long-term survival?'

TERMINAL CANCER

One of the saddest experiences I've come across happened when I was consulting a client who had been diagnosed with bowel and liver cancer. After her last surgery, two satellite tumors appeared where the incisions for the keyhole surgery had been made. From an Advanced Clearing Energetics point of view, this was an attack against the abdomen, and the tumors were a result of the body trying to protect the abdomen from further attacks. The thick lining of the abdomen called the peritoneum grew massively at the exact points where the incisions had been made.

However, my client never wanted that last operation and reported feeling ice cold just before she was put under the anesthetic. I believed this was the UDIN shock for the peritoneum and the signal for it to grow. What was so sad was that there was no evidence of bowel or liver cancer during the operation. She was clear of all those cancers but died from the effects of taking high doses of morphine to relieve the pain due to the satellite tumors.

In the last months of her life, she spent most of her time in a deep comatose sleep. She stopped eating and started to waste away. She was also boiling hot to the touch. After a couple of weeks she miraculously woke up. She came completely out of the deep, deep sleep and stopped taking the morphine. She wanted to get out of bed but had no energy to move. Her daughter told me that during this time her mother had long conversations with her family and was able to say many things that were very special for everyone concerned. Three days later, she went back into an even deeper sleep and sadly passed away a week later.

One of my students, Anne Sweet, one of the first hospice nurses in the UK, reports having seen this phenomenon many times as a nurse. She could never explain it until she realized that it was the Spike. She even mentioned that a few terminally ill clients had been through the Spike, fallen back into a deep sleep, and had slowly come out of this state feeling better, in the Rebuild Stage, wanting to eat, and their cancers had eventually disappeared. This is a very rare occurrence, but I have it on good authority from Anne that this does happen.

Parkinson's disease and shaking

Muscles go through involuntary twitching spasms and have the same electrical changes I mentioned earlier. The shaking of Parkinson's patients is thought to be caused by incorrect nerve impulses firing off in the brain. There is obviously a lot of electrical activity going on during this time. However, this does not explain why the symptoms disappear during sleep or under hypnosis.

We can go through what is called a 'suspended healing.' This is where the person is stuck in a section of the six stages. In Parkinson's, the person is stuck in the Spike. They then go through the Rebuild Stage, when they sleep or are in a deep rest. As you can see from the following diagram, the Stress Stage is repeated, the person rests, and during the Spike, they shake.

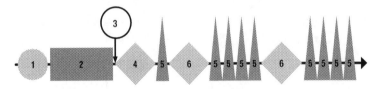

Key: the repeating Spike and Rebuild Stages of a Parkinson's patient

1 UDIN

2 Stress Stage

3 UDIN Reversal

4 Repair Stage

5 Spike

6 Rebuild Stage

The involuntary shaking of Parkinson's disease patients is due to the Spike being continually repeated during the day. The shaking stops during deep rest and sleep – the Rebuild Stage. In talking to Parkinson's patients, I found that the shaking gets worse or better on a day-to-day basis.

The Stress Stage recurs, which can be short and not shown in this diagram, and after a lull the shaking starts again. Sometimes, if the Stress Stage has been intense, the Spike will be more intense and therefore the shaking more violent. The Spike repeats itself over and over again. This is because clients have reminded themselves of the problem, unconsciously, time and time again, maybe for several years. The relay in the brain becomes scarred, and the person gets stuck in a repeat of the Spike.

PARKINSON'S DISEASE – INTENSE REGRETS

When I met John he was in his late 60s and had Parkinson's disease. His whole left arm would shake, with the main spasm acting as if he wanted to pull something close to him but couldn't quite get hold of whatever it was. Drinking a cup of tea was a challenge for him. His right foot would also twitch involuntarily; it was as if he wanted to move that foot forward but couldn't.

As the story of John's life started to unfold, I slowly got the answers to my questions as to why and how the hand and leg would shake, and why the way he presented himself was perceived as pitiable. John had been married for 40 years to the same woman, and he genuinely loved children. They didn't have any of their own, although he avoided telling me the reasons why.

He was right-wired, so the left-hand jerking had to do with a mother/son, child, or inner-world conflict; and his right foot had to do with an issue concerning his father, partner (his wife), or his outer world.

After probing a little, I discovered that John's Parkinson's had started in August 2000 when his wife caught him completely off guard by telling him that they would never have children and to stop even thinking about the possibility that she might change her mind. He was devastated, and he explained that every day he thought about what she said.

Unfortunately, I was never able to help John, as he first needed to work on solving the underlying problem.

Epileptic seizures

In both Parkinson's disease and epilepsy, we can see that there is an association that keeps the issue ongoing; it is being triggered every day or, in some instances, many times a day. That association can be the look of a person, the tone of someone's voice, or a place (such as work). It reminds the body of the original UDIN shock at an unconscious level, therefore causing the body to go through an ongoing cycle of repetitive healing.

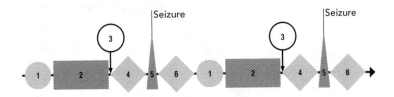

Key: the ongoing cycle of healing created by a repeating UDIN

1 UDIN   **4** Repair Stage

2 Stress Stage   **5** Spike

3 UDIN Reversal   **6** Rebuild Stage

With repeated Spikes, a person can have regular epileptic seizures, as the disease process just keeps repeating itself.

What I've found interesting regarding this phenomenon, as I have mentioned before, is that you can predict when the Spike will occur. It is often halfway between the Repair and the Rebuild Stages. However, as a rule of thumb, the length of the Stress Stage is the same as the Repair and Rebuild Stages combined. So if you know that the Stress Stage was active for two weeks, for example, the Repair Stage will also be active for one week, the Rebuild Stage another week. The Spike will then appear after the Repair Stage.

I've found these timings to be incredibly accurate; they allow Advanced Clearing Energetics practitioners to predict when the Spike will appear and also what the symptoms will be.

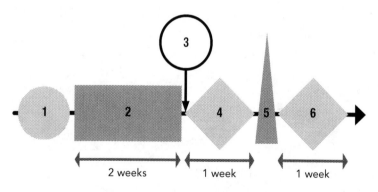

Key: predicting timings for the stages of disease

1 UDIN

2 Stress Stage

3 UDIN Reversal

4 Repair Stage

5 Spike

6 Rebuild Stage

If the Stress Stage lasts two weeks, then the Spike will occur after the Repair Stage has finished, in one week. The Rebuild Stage will take another week.

Examples of the six stages in action

As an example, I worked with a woman who came to see me concerning another problem, but asked me about an ear infection; it was bothering her and she wanted to know why it was there. She told me that she'd had a headache the day before, which had started at 11 a.m., and lasted until the afternoon – she hadn't taken any headache pills. This was a Spike. She explained that she felt very anxious and out of sorts during that time. She also told me the time when the earache started.

Knowing that the pain starts at the beginning of the Repair Stage, after the UDIN Reversal, I worked backward and asked her what had been going on at noon on Sunday. She told me she'd been out to a nightclub and her friend had commented the following morning that they were no longer 'spring chickens' and too old to be clubbing any longer. This had shocked her and caught her off guard – the UDIN. Her whole face lit up with rage as she remembered the tone of her friend's voice. My client was single and in her early 30s and, despite being beautiful, felt in competition with younger women when it came to finding a mate. This was something she had not wanted to hear; she knew it deep down, but she had been denying it to herself.

I then asked her what had happened a week later, the UDIN Reversal. She told me that she had apologized to her friend, and made a decision to start looking for a man in situations that were more befitting her age, for example, dinner parties or social engagements. It was at this point that the earache appeared and she went into the Repair Stage. I then worked out exactly how much longer the earache would last and sure enough, she called a few days later and said that the ache had completely gone.

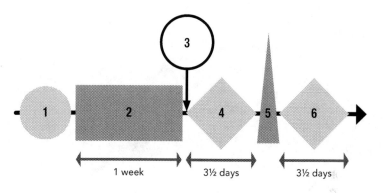

Key: stages and timings of an ear infection

1 UDIN

2 Stress Stage

3 UDIN Reversal

4 Repair Stage

5 Spike

6 Rebuild Stage

The UDIN occurred when her friend made the rude comment to her, and her earache occurred following the UDIN Reversal, during the Repair Stage, which lasted three and a half days. Following her headache, the Rebuild Stage lasted another three and a half days.

I went through this myself a few years ago when I had to complete a project for a training course. In order to meet the required deadline, I realized I'd have to work through the night. This was something I didn't want to do; I literally couldn't digest it, but had no other option. This was the UDIN. I worked through the evening and late into the night, but was extremely stressed and anxious about completing the project (Stress Stage). Amazingly, I finished everything earlier than I thought, at 4 a.m. (UDIN Reversal).

I went to bed totally relieved and slept well. I was hot in bed and sweated quite a lot – the Repair Stage. When I woke up the next day at 10 a.m., I felt 'out of sorts' in my belly and knew something wasn't right, and 30 minutes later suffered the first of several intense bouts of diarrhea that lasted until 1 p.m. (the Spike). I then felt really tired and hungry, so I ate some food (Rebuild Stage). I attended a meeting in the afternoon, and afterward was exhausted but otherwise felt okay, and then slept until 8 p.m. When I awoke I felt fine, and then went to bed at my usual time and slept well.

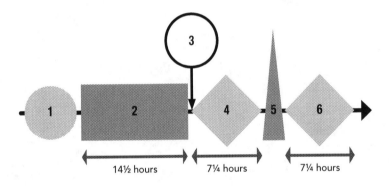

Key: stages and timings of a bacterial infection

1 UDIN	4 Repair Stage
2 Stress Stage	5 Spike
3 UDIN Reversal	6 Rebuild Stage

The UDIN moment was a decision I couldn't digest – I then worked through the night. The work took me until 4 a.m., and so resolved the issue (UDIN Reversal). I slept deeply until 10 a.m. but awoke with stomach cramps, and diarrhea started 30 minutes later and lasted for an hour and a half, the Spike. I then rested until 8 p.m., ate a meal, and went to bed as usual.

In the past, I'd have blamed the gut issue on the food I'd eaten or a bug; however, in understanding this process as simply the body's way of resolving a UDIN, I can relax, and let my body do what it needs to do, without resorting to drugs or obsessing about bugs and viruses, etc.

Emergency medicine

However, just understanding the symptoms and the healing Spike doesn't mean the issue isn't life-threatening in certain instances, and then emergency medicine is brilliant at dealing with the effects of the intense reactions to different parts of the six stages. We can see this in the diagram below.

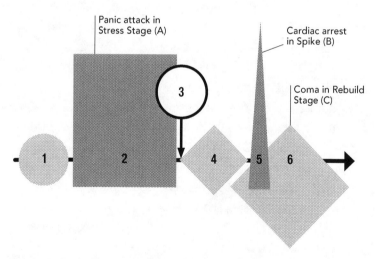

Key: intense symptoms can create the need for emergency care

1 UDIN	**4** Repair Stage
2 Stress Stage	**5** Spike
3 UDIN Reversal	**6** Rebuild Stage

During the Stress Stage, the intensity of the symptoms becomes life-threatening, as in a severe panic attack (point A). In the Spike, the person can experience extremely intense symptoms such as high blood pressure or a cardiac arrest (point B). In the Repair or Rebuild Stages, the person can dip into a coma (point C).

Here we have the six stages. There are times when, during these stages, the issue can become dangerous and the person needs immediate medical care. In the Stress Stage, patients can become so stressed that they may have a panic attack or become violent and dangerous to others. For example, I had a client whose complications stemmed from the fact that she had not slept in more than eight days. Such imbalances in the brain are common, especially with people with mental health disorders. In the Repair and Rebuild Stages, the issue can represent itself when the patient dips too low into these stages; this could result in a person going into a coma or organs shutting down.

As regards life-threatening issues in the Spike, we can see in the diagram that there are instances that require immediate medical attention. These include issues such as a violent seizure that doesn't subside after a few minutes, and a stroke where the blood vessels in the brain are damaged by the pressure build-up caused by the Spike, which in turn causes blood to flow into brain cavities, damaging parts of the brain and resulting in brain damage.

There are instances where the resulting glial cells (brain repairing cells) in the brain relays, which form in the Repair/Rebuild Stage, swell so much that it causes pressure in the brain; this results in the ventricles, which regulate fluid in the brain, becoming blocked. This is called 'hydroencephalitis' and can result in extensive brain damage or even death without medical attention. Other serious results of the Spike include cardiac arrest, extreme diarrhea (where the person dehydrates due to the loss of so much liquid), and bursting of vessels in the body (with life-threatening consequences, such as a bowel splitting, resulting in poisoning).

There are many things that can go wrong in the Spike, and emergency medicine is designed to deal with such complications. I'm certain you can appreciate how important emergency care is when dealing with such issues.

Knowing when to go to a hospital for emergency care is a tricky question. I always err on the side of caution: getting advice from a doctor in the first place and then going to the ER if required.

How drugs and lifestyle factors affect the healing process

Without many drugs, people could die or their lives could become severely hampered. My interest is in how drugs affect the six stages, so if you're on medication for a particular disease or issue, it's worth doing a bit of research into what each drug does and its side effects. In my opinion, sometimes the cocktail of drugs can be more debilitating and more stressful than the original problem.

Reducing the number or combination taken needs to be discussed with a qualified medical practitioner, but it does not need to be your present practitioner. Advice concerning the combination of what you are taking is vital, as doctors can't possibly know how every drug will be affected by another drug.

Continually drinking coffee, smoking, and working in a fast-moving job can have the same effect as drugs. Our body can take this stress, but it does need to repair itself, hence the reason people often find themselves unwell as soon as they slow down on weekends or on vacation. I know of people who get terrible sneezing fits, have insomnia for a few hours at night as soon as the weekend arrives, or have minor bouts of diarrhea. All of these issues are symptoms of the Spike.

A friend who is also a medical doctor explained to me one day that the body could survive on 40 percent of its optimum functionality. This explains how people can abuse their bodies for years, but as soon as they stop, they get really ill and some end up in the hospital. As an extreme example, people who retire from high-pressure jobs then go on to have a cardiac arrest (the Spike of the coronary or pulmonary arteries). The worst is the pulmonary embolism or the silent killer, as there are often very few symptoms that let people know they have a problem.

Understanding heart problems

From an Advanced Clearing Energetics perspective, there are two types of cardiac arrest. The first is due to the Spike of the myocardium (the cardiac muscle of the heart) – a myocardial infarction. The reaction is the same as that of a muscle in the body and is linked embryonically to the middle brain (cerebral medulla). During the Spike, the muscle (heart) cramps and sometimes stops. It can be started again using a defibrillator, but the original stressful cause is due to the person feeling defeated. Once the heart has been restarted, the person normally returns to full health. The heart muscle is rarely damaged, but like any muscle in the body that is in the Rebuild Stage, it will look different and under a biopsy will look diseased, although from my perspective, it means the organ is just in a rebuild state.

The second type is related to the coronary arteries. The cause of the cardiac arrest is due to losing to someone else; or losing something that you own, such as a house, your job, or a partner. The arteries in the Stress Stage go through a cell reduction, and the inner lining of the cell wall becomes thinner. After the UDIN Reversal, the arteries then repair and the cell wall gets thicker. This is due to a build-up of plaque called cholesterol. If the length of the Stress Stage continues for many months and is very intense, then in the Repair Stage the build-up of plaque in the arteries can be so great that it restricts the blood flow, which means that the muscle doesn't get enough blood, which might be noticed during exercise or intense activity.

After the Repair Stage, the arteries go through a Spike. The plaque that has built up on the inside is shed, then passes into the bloodstream and is processed by the liver.

However, if this plaque build-up is large, then it breaks away, forming a blood clot, which can prevent blood getting to the heart muscles. This results in a cardiac arrest, causing part of those muscles to die. If too much muscle is affected, then the heart will stop pumping and the person will die. Trying to restart the heart in this instance is often futile since the muscle is already damaged beyond repair.

In nature we see this in deer. A stag that loses his harem to a younger stag in a fight will then go and find another harem. If, after nine months, he is unsuccessful, he is deemed no longer worthy of maintaining a herd, and therefore useless. The territory is lost, the stag will then go into the Repair Stage, and during the Spike the cardiac arrest will be fatal.

This happens in people in a similar way. If our territory is invaded or we no longer have a territory to maintain, then the ensuing Spike can be fatal, if the length of time has been almost a year. Take, for example, a man who retires from a high-powered job, then comes into a household where the woman runs the house. She is the boss (especially after menopause, which can make a woman react more territorially). He loses his position. If this situation isn't resolved, then there is some likelihood that the man may look for another mate or have a cardiac arrest.

Obviously there are other factors, too, that can cause cardiac arrest. People who go into stressful jobs, where their position is continually being invaded and work pressures are intense, seem to be more likely to develop heart disease. The combination of this together with certain foods and lifestyle habits (e.g., lack of exercise, smoking, etc.) is also likely to lead to heart disease and accelerate this process. It is no wonder that these people are more prone to heart disease than others. As they relax and go into the Repair Stage, the body deposits plaque on the interior walls of the arteries. If you keep repeating this process, then the plaque builds up and the heart muscles receive less oxygen, resulting in ongoing issues. The medical solution is a heart bypass, where blood vessels are taken, usually from the leg, to replace the damaged vessels. Undoubtedly this procedure saves many lives.

However, contrary to belief, I am convinced that the actual cause of the disease is territorial in men and social in women – not bad foods, alcoholic drinks, lack of exercise, or smoking. Although these stress-related habits do go on to make the whole situation worse, they are not the causes of heart disease. This explains why completely healthy people can develop heart disease – people who don't smoke (and never have), who have really good-quality diets, who don't drink, and who exercise regularly. It also explains why some people who do the total opposite live to a ripe old age with no heart problems. I believe the real killer is the shock, which causes the disease process in the first place, and not dealing with it, or not allowing the appropriate time and space to fully recuperate. Recognizing when we are in the Stress Stage is the key.

The problem is that many people don't recognize the Stress Stage or that there might be the potential for a serious issue to occur. In the Stress Stage we feel fine – no aches, no pains, no infections, and we have the sharpness of mind and energy to deal with problems. For example, a fellow trainer told me that, as a runner, he ran so much better after an argument with his wife, especially one that dragged on for weeks. This also explains why we need to look after ourselves when it comes to eating healthily and exercising regularly. What isn't mentioned is the need to spend time relaxing and taking time out just for us, as every alternative and complementary practitioner would intuitively tell you. Sports therapists worked this out years ago; the body needs time to heal after intensive exercise. Time off to let your body heal is as important as the time you put into training.

The reason we need to relax, and I mean really take time out to heal, is simple. If we keep putting the body under continuous strain, it will eventually need to repair itself anyway. The other problem that occurs in these instances is that if the body continually experiences pressure, then the chances of reacting to a minor problem in a major way is increased. Just think about how you react to things when you're lacking sleep compared to when you have had enough sleep.

Myalgic encephalomyelitis (ME) or chronic fatigue syndrome

The opposite of being caught in the Stress Stage occurs when a person experiences an ongoing cycle of the Repair/ Rebuild Stages with a repetitive healing Spike. Take, for example, ME (also known as chronic fatigue syndrome). Most ME sufferers become unwell after an illness, often a bout of flu. If, during the Spike, the person goes through another UDIN moment, this can become associated with the whole disease process, and the person continually loops through the second half of the disease process. This is what we call a 'suspended healing,' and is demonstrated by what happened to one of my clients.

After moving, because the next-door neighbor had been aggressive and violent toward him and his family, my client had an intense bronchial viral infection, resulting in him being laid up in bed with influenza symptoms – the Repair Stage.

During the Repair Stage, his wife accused him of merely having 'man flu,' and this created a UDIN moment. It was unexpected, dramatic, isolating, and he had no strategy for dealing with his wife's criticism. Subsequently her face and voice became associated with the Repair Stage.

My client was in the Repair Stage when a second UDIN occurred (when his wife shocked him); this second UDIN locked him into a suspended healing that led to chronic fatigue syndrome.

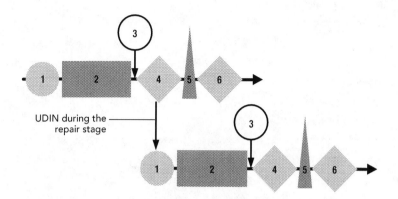

Key: UDIN during the repair stage causes a second cycle of disease

1 UDIN   **4** Repair Stage

2 Stress Stage   **5** Spike

3 UDIN Reversal   **6** Rebuild Stage

This UDIN moment started another disease process, and meant he was in the Stress Stage of a new disease process *and* the Repair Stage of the flu disease process. He was stuck in the Repair Stage still needing to recuperate but stressed from the new UDIN, which was due to his wife's comments. So although he was in the Repair Stage of the flu, he experienced a combination of the Stress and Repair Stages at the same time – he was awake but had no energy. Given time, this process would normally resolve itself, but when you add the trigger of his wife's face and voice putting him back into the Stress Stage daily, you can see how the whole process kept going around and around. He told me that he felt stressed when his wife was around, and exhausted when she wasn't there.

My client slept erratically (often a symptom of ME), and dreamt a tremendous amount. He told me he would often wake up feeling more exhausted than he did before he went to bed. Here we can see the Spike at work. Upon waking up, his body would have gone into the Rebuild Stage. Then his wife would unconsciously trigger the second conflict again by looking at him or saying something to him, which would create stress. Then she would go to work and he would end up with no energy as he went into the Repair Stage yet again – a combination of the Repair Stage and the Stress Stage triggered by his wife. Then, when he went to bed, the Spike would repeat itself continually, causing restless sleep and leaving him feeling exhausted the next day as he went into the Rebuild Stage. The whole cycle would repeat itself day and night over and over again.

My client recognized how the disease process worked and that he was stuck in a suspended healing, so I worked with him, teaching him to remove the associations. He did some great work in clearing out the problem, but then went into a full-blown Repair Stage where he had mild pneumonia, and was prescribed antibiotics. The antibiotics probably slowed down his recovery, but he is now on the mend and doing voluntary work three days a week. He tells me that he is feeling much better, though not totally on form. The pneumonia was probably a repeat of the original symptoms, since he said that it had occurred after he resolved everything in his mind that had to do with his wife.

However, I believe that he hasn't fully recovered because he chooses not to. That might sound harsh, but my client likes spending more time with his child, away from a job that he dislikes, and it suits his wife, too.

The path of least resistance

The body and the unconscious mind are intelligent, and the way the mind–body connection works allows us to follow the path of least resistance. You know how hard it is to stop a habit – something you enjoy in the moment of indulgence, even though you know it is bad for you in the long term – e.g., smoking, recreational drugs, cream cakes, etc. We therefore have to put a lot of energy into changing old established patterns. Most ME sufferers do eventually come out of their patterns, but it takes something pretty major to shake them out of their comfort zone back into reality. Usually it is a change in environmental or social circumstances that removes the triggers from the person, stopping the suspended healing.

There can also be other factors involved that can stop a person from returning to health. These can revolve around the overall energy of the person being inhibited by other erroneous factors, the main ones being toxicity and a high loading of parasites and, more recently, genetically modified foods. In this instance, again the body is being held in a suspended healing. Parasites and toxicity can all be eliminated from the body, but it takes energy to do so. If you're in a Repair or Rebuild Stage, all the energy is being directed toward healing the main issue. Parasites need energy to live, so they take it away from the host, causing the whole system to be out of balance. Genetically modified foods can be eliminated from your diet, and this is highly recommended even if you are healthy.[4]

In this chapter we've discussed the Spike in depth. This strange 'Spike' is thought to be a biological test, and the point where water, together with cells and bacteria built up during the Repair Stage, are eliminated not only from the organ but also from the affected brain relay. This 'Spike' explains the symptoms of many diseases and why there are complications during this time. The Spike is responsible for so much pain and so much anguish, but the truth is we now know why it is there and, with enough information, we can predict when it is likely to occur and seek medical advice if it becomes life-threatening.

We have now turned a disease from being static into a moving process. This is the difference between owning a disease and running a disease process. A person is not his or her disease. It does not define anyone. The disease is rather a 'lower level' function, a process that the body goes through in order to heal itself.

In the next chapter, we'll discuss the link between the brain and the organs, discover where a stressful event gets stuck in our brains, and why specific types of conflicts affect us in different organs in differing ways. We'll also look at what goes on in our brains and how there is an elegant system of relays that switch on and off in line with the six stages.

CHAPTER 8

OUR BRAIN – THE BIOLOGICAL RELAY SWITCH AND RECORDER OF EVERY DISEASE

'In proportion to our body mass, our brain is three times as large as that of our nearest relatives. This huge organ is dangerous and painful to give birth to, expensive to build and, in a resting human, uses about 20 percent of the body's energy even though it is just 2 percent of the body's weight. There must be some reason for all this evolutionary expense.'

Dr. Susan Blakemore, author of 'Me, Myself, I,'
New Scientist, March 13, 1999

I've been fascinated by health for many years and introduced to many different disciplines in my time, but the thing that really amazes me is brain CT scan reading. Suddenly, here was an area previously limited to a few select doctors, which allowed a trained individual to get an accurate picture of what was happening energetically inside a person's mind and, as Birgitte's story illustrates, it is a very powerful tool.

CHRONIC LACK OF ENERGY – LACK OF CONTROL

Birgitte complained that she had 'absolutely no energy.' She constantly felt tired and sleepy; the only thing keeping on her feet was sheer willpower. She knew she didn't have chronic fatigue syndrome (Epstein Barr) or ME, but she also knew that something wasn't right.

Birgitte's story started when she worked on a cultural–historical farm, where everything was done in the same way as it had been done in the 1940s. She recounted how immensely fit she felt and how much energy she had. She loved her work but not the shared accommodations, so she managed to secure an apartment elsewhere on the farm where she could be alone. During this time she met and fell in love with someone ten years younger, and then became pregnant. Sadly, she suffered a miscarriage a few weeks into the pregnancy, but the scan showed an incomplete miscarriage, and she was advised to have a vacuum aspiration at the local hospital to complete the process.

At the hospital, she negotiated with the nurse not to be given a general anesthetic, and the chief nurse saw that Birgitte was capable of relaxing her body enough for the procedure. She did, however, have a local anesthetic. Everything was fine until the doctor started the procedure, which involved a machine that sounded like a very loud vacuum cleaner.

All the blood went from her head. She kept thinking, 'I cannot move because I will get hurt.' She recounted, 'I can't pass out or faint because this was the decision I made, I went all into my head.' After the experience, she just suppressed the whole thing and got back into shape very quickly.

However, after a few weeks, Birgitte noticed a dull ache in her kidneys. Realizing this could be more than a minor problem, she dropped everything and sought medical advice, and was diagnosed with a renal pelvis infection. She had a very high fever and a horrendous sharp pain in the kidneys, like a knife that was constantly there. Later on she found out that she was passing kidney stones. She moved in with her mother during these five weeks.

In the last stages of her healing, her boyfriend came to see her and told her that she could now no longer have the apartment and that there was nowhere else for her to live on the farm. This was another shock, and she now felt that she had nowhere to go. After being told this, she went into a deep depression, which resulted in her staying more or less in bed for a month and a half. The only person she saw during this time was her boyfriend, and she became pregnant again. Still depressed, she had the child, thinking it would solve the depression, but instead she felt trapped, more imprisoned, and she could not get out of this horrible state.

Eventually she moved in with her boyfriend, and for three and a half years she battled with the depression. Although she deeply loved her boyfriend, he could no longer deal with her issues, and eventually they split up. Unexpectedly, the depression lifted at this time, but the lack of energy she had been experiencing got worse.

If you met Birgitte, you would have no idea that she was suffering in this way, but when I studied her CT scan I saw small ring markings that I knew related to specific organs in the body (to see the CT scan, visit www.whyamisick.com). Not only was I able to show her the two shocks that caused her depression, I was also able to point out organs where there had been a problem. An example was an old digestive issue, whereupon she explained that she'd had a problem due to a friend of hers having gone mad and disappearing for weeks.

However, the most dramatic thing I found that made complete sense to Birgitte was when I asked her if she had a problem with her thyroid. She replied that she didn't. Then I showed her how the area in the front left-hand side of the brain in the cortex area had a speckled ring, which meant that this was in the Rebuild Stage and that it was a suspended healing. I consulted with a doctor friend, and he explained that the symptoms of this issue were a lack of energy and always feeling tired, commonly known as an underactive thyroid.

I explained that we could clear the energy around the event that caused the issue to occur, one of feeling powerless, and doing that would mean the thyroid would return to normal function, her tiredness would disappear, and her energy would return.

I asked her to put together a history of her medical issues. That evening she wrote four pages of notes and worked out what had caused the UDIN; it was at the point of the procedure where she felt powerless, *listening to the machine and feeling terrified to move. The next day we cleared the UDIN moment and the underlying trapped energy. Immediately she felt better, and over the course of the next few days the tiredness completely disappeared and her energy returned.*

To explain Birgitte's condition in more detail, a relay switches on in the brain on the front, left-hand side of the gray matter (cortex). This relay relates to the thyroglossal ducts; these are the tubes that allow the thyroid hormones to be released into the blood. These ducts become bigger, thereby allowing the two thyroid gland hormones to be released into the system so that they can flow faster into the bloodstream. These two hormones, thyroxin and triiodothyronine, regulate the metabolism in a person (basically how quickly a person burns energy and makes proteins).

The overall effect of this widening of the ducts allows people to react faster so they can deal with whatever it is they feel powerless against (in Birgitte's case, the painful and noisy procedure). Once the stress resolves itself, then the ducts repair themselves, they get smaller, and so fewer of the thyroid hormones enter the bloodstream; less thyroid hormone means less energy.

Energy and the mind–body connection

Is there a mind–body connection? Could the medical profession be missing one of the most obvious links there is to disease by focusing only on biochemistry to heal people?

It may or may not be obvious, but there is no doubt that there is a massive amount of biochemistry going on.

Neuropeptides rush through the mind, which then tells the body to react in a specific way. This is well understood scientifically, and the simple proof of this biochemical reaction and connection is the effect that a positive or negative thought has on a person's body posture, breathing, or blood chemistry.

Proof of this is simple. Take depression as an example, which affects a people's blood chemistry by lowering the amount of serotonin in the brain and the body. The reduction in this hormone affects both breathing and posture: e.g., their behavior will change as they look at the world, act, walk, and talk very differently. Energy levels also reduce in depression sufferers, as they tend to spend a lot of time doing nothing, and nothing seems to interest them.[1]

We can see the effects of lifting depression by the use of drugs such as Prozac, the first anti-depression drug of its class. Within three weeks of taking the drug, most people suffering with depression do feel better.

Even if the drug is designed to do something completely different, such as a beta-blocker (used to reduce high blood pressure), it can have a massive shift in our way of thinking. Therefore, I think it is safe to say that what we think is linked to our biochemistry, which in turn is linked to our emotions, and vice versa. What I'm saying here is neither radical nor new, although I find it strange that the medical profession doesn't acknowledge this blatantly obvious mind–body connection.

Another area that the medical profession conveniently ignores is energy, even though the existence of energy can easily be proven. You may remember from chemistry lessons in school that during a chemical reaction heat is emitted, and heat is energy. Consider our neural pathways: they use electrical energy to communicate throughout the mind and the body, switching on nerve impulses releasing neurotransmitters into the system. This is a chemical reaction; therefore, heat is produced.

We can't see nerve electrical energy, but it is the same transference of energy that we use to power an electric light bulb, admittedly with less current flowing through it. So it's safe to say that when we think, we produce heat energy changes, which fire off electrical energy changes along with biochemical reactions, resulting in changes throughout the mind and body. Electrical waves are also responsible for considerable changes in the mind and body, which the medical profession has partly ignored although, to a degree, they have been using them for decades.

It isn't difficult to prove that electrical waves surround us; our brains and organs, and those in turn receive and emit electrical waves. Consider the non-invasive use of electro-encephalograph (EEG) that measures brain waves or electrocardiograph (ECG) that measures heart waves, thereby proving that we emit waves through changes in our thinking. We can also stimulate muscles using non-invasive techniques. For example, a TENS machine, which involves placing pads on the skin instead of needles in the body (as in acupuncture) can be used to relieve pain and illustrates that the human body can receive electrical waves.

Some interesting experiments conducted by scientists confirm the fact that we produce electrical waves. They invented a skullcap that contained an array of 64 electrodes. Using special computer algorithms, they demonstrated how people could control a cursor on a computer screen using only thought.[2] The technology has advanced so quickly that you can even buy one of these machines for the same price as a laptop or tablet computer (http://www.emotiv.com/), now with considerably fewer electrodes.

I think we can, therefore, assume that the brain and organs emit and receive electrical information that, in turn, creates a field around them. This information is emitted and received via the nerves, which are embedded in every part of our body and every organ. As soon as an electrical current is passed through a wire, an electrical field is produced – this field is thought to interact with everything around and inside you. Recent research by Professor Peter Fraser has shown that the heart links to the brain and the nervous system, and the work of other people and organizations such as the Heart Math Institute in California support his findings.[3] The heart seems to contain 65 to 75 percent neuronal cells. It seems that as the heart beats, it emits an electrical wave, imprinting information into the blood passing through it, changing the biochemistry in the mind and body.

The fact that we create a field around us is nothing new, as the police and emergency services have been using specially designed thermal-imaging cameras for many years to track criminals and for search and rescue. However, it's worth mentioning because it is just more evidence that there is a mind–body connection; thoughts alters our energy. Emotions are thoughts, and these also change our state – our biochemistry. All of these seemingly separate elements, which make us what we are, are not separate; they are totally integrated.

Thinking, emotions, and disease

Why this is so important is because the medical profession has separated thinking, and therefore emotions, from disease. If doctors believed that a thought was connected to the way the body reacted, then they would reconsider the effect that a medical diagnosis has on a person, especially one with such implications as a diagnosis of cancer. It is not only the doctors that need to be wary of this; alternative and complementary practitioners do as well. During an evaluation or medical diagnosis of any kind, people are in a heightened state of awareness, and this can have a dramatic effect on how they perceive what they have been told. People are in a trance state, and when they are given a horrific or challenging medical diagnosis, they can and often do go into a UDIN.

Looking specifically at traditional medicine, we find that research is reductionist in nature. The researchers don't look at the mind and the body; they look at an individual cell and dismantle it, and rip it apart in order to find out what's going wrong inside a diseased cell. Then they develop drugs that alter the chemistry in this single cell, thereby repairing or destroying the constitution of the cell. Remember, the researchers work with diseased cells in isolation, omitting the environment and the mental state of the person.

If you disagree, then just consider what effect chemotherapy has on any replicating cell. No consideration is given to side effects since, from a reductionist viewpoint, side effects are an inconvenient by-product. No consideration is given to the person's state of the mind, since the theory is that the chemotherapy drugs only destroy the cancer cells, but as any cancer patient who has had chemotherapy will tell you, the side effects are horrendous. Physical side effects of chemotherapy often cause patients to lose their hair, together with other cells that are replicating, such as nails. The psychological side effects cause loss of self-esteem, mood shifts, irritability, depression, low sex drive, and changes in how the patient thinks about him- or herself as a person. Even taste and smell change while taking these drugs, and immense nausea is regularly reported to be felt by patients.[4]

Post-traumatic stress disorder (PTSD)

As a person goes through a UDIN, the effect of the emotion that occurs gets trapped in the system (see page 72). We can easily prove that emotions get stored in our neurological system. Just think of a happy event from the past, and for most people the emotions reappear. They are in there somewhere and they are often easily accessible; with a UDIN, the emotion gets trapped in the system in the same way.

Research carried out in 2005 in the USA at Duke University's Center for Cognitive Neuroscience, Department of Psychological and Brain Sciences, and Brain Imaging and Analysis Center found that people who experience a traumatic event get trapped in a cycle of emotion and recall, and in particular they studied post-traumatic stress disorder (PTSD).

The effects of a UDIN produce the same reaction as that of a person who experiences PTSD. In essence they are very similar, if not the same. The types of events that affect people with PTSD are horrendous: accidents, death, war events, or horrific fires. Many of the people who suffer from this type of psychological disorder are soldiers, paramedics, and firefighters.

By using functional magnetic resonance imaging (fMRI), a relatively new and complex imaging technique that uses magnetism and radio waves to see inside the body, researchers were able to establish that as a person reassesses the memories of a horrific event, it shows up in the brain and, specifically, in the area for processing emotional memories – the amygdala and the hippocampus. These events were trapped and the pictures and emotions were caught in a continuous loop. What was different about this research was the time delay that the researchers used to assess their clients' recall. In previous experiments, the time difference had only been minutes, but in this research the time difference was a year.[5]

Why this is significant is because people suffering from PTSD are affected mentally and physically by the event that shocked them. They not only have severe psychological changes, but are found to suffer from heart-related problems, respiratory system-related problems, digestive problems, reproductive system-related problems, diabetes, arthritis, and pain, all of which suggest a direct, provable scientific link between a specific stressful event and specific diseases.

Not surprisingly from an Advanced Clearing Energetics perspective, the medical professions interpretation of the known causes for these diseases in people with PTSD is not known. It postulates that the stress these people go through affects the body, increasing the risk of problems and illness.[6]

Disease and conflicts related to PTSD

In order to understand the types of conflicts to which each disease is related, I have listed them here:

Disease or issue	Related conflict
Coronary heart disease	Loss of something important such as a house or one's job. One's territory.
Respiratory system-related problems (bronchial and laryngeal mucosa)	Being scared of an impending attack by someone. A territorial fear conflict.
Digestive problems (stomach, liver, gallbladder, and pancreas mucosa)	Feeling angry because someone has taken something away from you. A territorial anger conflict.
Digestive problems (digestive tract)	Something that couldn't be digested e.g., an event that sits in the gut and can't be accepted.
Diabetes type 1 – hyperglycemia (beta islet cells, insulin injecting)	Resisting change or defending yourself from someone.
Diabetes type 2 – hypoglycemia (alpha islet cells, controlled by diet)	Being scared of something disgusting.
Arthritis	Severe separation from others and a lack of value for oneself.
Pain	Most probably to do with the kidney collecting tubules, feeling abandoned, and another disease going through its Repair/Rebuild Stages.
Reproductive system-related problems (ovaries and testicles)	Profound loss.

All of these issues are seen in people suffering with PTSD, which means there might be evidence that a neurological dysfunction (known to affect the brain and a person's behavior), is linked to specific diseases. Therefore, a specific stressful event affects the brain in a specific location, which then affects a specific organ for a biological reason. Further evidence demonstrates this can be seen in MRIs of PTSD[7] sufferers who show activity in specific areas of the brain.

Brain imaging techniques have also found that there is a direct link between specific areas of the brain and movement associated with Parkinson's disease.[8] Further evidence that the primary and motor cortex of the brain are responsible for basic movement has also been established.[9]

Embryology

As well as many experiments relating to brain imaging and specific organs in the body, most of the studies relate to movement or diseases that affect neural pathways in the body, such as Parkinson's and MS. There is also research that indicates the locations of specific areas of the brain and their relationship to specific organs of the body.

For example, in the 1950s, Wilder Penfield worked with epileptic patients in an attempt to assist them in stopping their seizures. He carried out experiments, during open brain surgery, where the patients had been given a localized anesthetic, meaning they were awake and could speak to the surgeon. Using an electrical probe on certain areas of the cortex of the brain, he could stimulate specific areas of the body. Wilder Penfield established that the brain was organized in a beautiful system and that the brain was crossed, meaning that by stimulating the left-hand side of the brain, the right-hand side of the body was affected, and vice versa. (To do a fun experiment of brain probing in the sensory cortex, go to www.pbs.org/wgbh/aso/tryit/brain/.)

Modern brain mapping has defined various areas of the brain and their related functions, and it appears that the brain is connected to the body in an elegantly organized system. Each part of the body and each organ has a connection to a specific area of the brain. For example, the area responsible for visual processing is at the back of the brain – you do, literally, have eyes in the back of your head. Sound is processed in the side lobes of the brain. The sensory areas, responsible for touch, are located at the top of the brain.

This type of brain mapping is relatively old and only covers the cortex of the brain. There is, however, an area that is well understood but ignored to some extent when it comes to our design as humans, and this is the link between specific organs and areas of the brain. To understand this we need to look at embryology, which is taught for about four days in medical school but from then on appears to be ignored by the medical profession, unless someone chooses to specialize in premature babies.

To explain this link we need to understand the basic fundamentals of embryology: what is happening in the womb from the point of conception to developing into a human being. Humans start off as a single cell that divides into 50 trillion cells, which then develop to make a grown adult. Within the first 30 days, three specific layers of cells develop – the endoderm, mesoderm, and ectoderm – confusingly known as 'germ' layers and, although they have nothing to do with germs and microbes, they do link beautifully to how we react in the Repair/Rebuild Stages of the disease process to fungi, bacteria, and viruses (see also page 187).

Each one of these layers makes up specific parts of various organs. The endoderm (inner layer) is responsible for our digestive system, which runs from the mouth to the anus, and includes the meat (parenchyma) of the liver and parenchyma of the pancreas plus the lung alveoli. The collecting tubules of the kidneys can also be found in the brain stem and are responsible for regulating the stored water throughout our system. (Note: The kidney collecting tubules develop from the mesoderm area of the brain and are not endoderm-directed organs.)

The mesoderm (middle layer) is the thick leathery skin of the body. It is the dermis area of the skin, which surrounds and protects the inner organs. The pericardium is a thick layer of skin surrounding the heart. The peritoneum covers the digestive organs, including the liver, and the pleura surrounds the lungs. The mammary glands are also directed by the mesoderm – the middle layer of the brain. Here, we also find the skeleton, striated muscles, the heart muscle, tendons, teeth, and cartilage. The smooth muscles of the intestine, stomach, and esophagus are also situated here.

The outer layer, the ectoderm, is responsible for the sensory organs. These connect us with the outside world. The most obvious is the outer layer of the skin known as the epidermis. We also have the mucosa, the slimy areas of our system, responsible for preventing our organs from drying out, and for giving us vital sensory feedback in order for us to function successfully and survive in our environment. The nasal mucosa is here (smell), the bronchi and laryngeal mucosa, the gall bladder ducts, liver mucosa, stomach mucosa, duodenum mucosa, and pancreas mucosa.

Interestingly, we find the coronary arteries and veins in the cortex, as well as the alpha and beta islet cells of the pancreas and the thyroglossal ducts and pharyngeal gland. We also find the seeing part of our eyes – mainly the retina and vitreous fluid – the hearing part of our ears, and the upper part of our skin, movement, touch and other sensory information of our body.

So, as we develop from the single fertilized cell, we divide into the three germ layers. At the same time each germ layer is connected to a specific area of the nervous system and brain. The endoderm is connected to the brain stem. The mesoderm is connected to the cerebellum – at the back of the brain – and is responsible for the thick skins surrounding our organs – and is also connected to the white matter. The cerebral medulla, which is responsible for support, therefore includes our muscles and skeleton. The ectoderm is connected to the cerebral cortex and hence the sensory organs that connect us to the outside world.

Our understanding of how embryology and the constitution of the brain are linked by a simple map of the organs has been mostly ignored. The thesis that I'm about to explain has, as yet, only some scientific verification, but the evidence seems to point to the constitution of the body reflecting perfectly in embryology and brain layers. So, if, for example, people suffering from PTSD are more likely to suffer from heart-related problems, respiratory system-related problems, digestive problems, reproductive system-related problems, diabetes, arthritis, and pain than someone who has not experienced PTSD, then there is probably a link to the ongoing stressful emotions they experience.

This means that if each separate area of the body and the brain is connected through embryology, then looking at the organ that is affected from an embryological point of view, you would see this obvious link. The ongoing stressful event shows up in the brain in a specific area that corresponds to the organ that is affected, but not the whole organ, just the specific embryonic layer. Take, for example, the lung that is made out of two embryonic layers. The alveoli are connected to the endoderm (inner layer) and therefore the brain stem, and the bronchi mucosa to the ectoderm (outer layer) and therefore the cortex. Two completely different embryonic layers are showing up in two completely different areas of the brain, but from the point of view of the medical profession, it is still the lungs.

Going back to the brain–body connection, let us explore the basic premise that seems to drive each embryonic level.

Endoderm (inner layer)

This relates to the brain stem; practically all the parts of the organs found in this endoderm embryonic layer have to do with digestion. The types of stressful events that affect this layer are an inability to digest something a person has seen or heard – for example, being told you're a liar when clearly you're not. Diseases that occur here are designed to help us digest these issues more effectively by increasing the surface area of the digestive tract or organ affected, thereby allowing better absorption of whatever it was that got stuck. This occurs in the Stress Stage.

Mesoderm (middle area)

This relates to two areas, the first one being the cerebellum; the stressful events that cause this layer to react are to do with an impending attack against us. An example would be imminent surgery on the intestines thickening the peritoneum. Diseases that occur in this first part of the mesoderm are designed to protect our inner organs from attack by thickening the leathery skin layer in the Stress Stage. Another example worth considering is facial acne, indicating an attack against who we are, e.g., losing face. Skin builds up in the first stage and then is eaten away by bacteria in the Repair/Rebuild Stages, hence the pimple and pus that is squeezed out from this point.

An issue relating to us not supporting ourselves, or not receiving support from others, would affect out skeletal and muscular system, and would therefore show up in the mesoderm part of the brain (the cerebral medulla). An example would be letting people walk all over you because you don't value yourself at a deep level. The cartilage in the lumbar vertebrae becomes stronger following the resolution of the stressful event in the Repair/Rebuild Stages. Diseases in this second part of the mesoderm are designed to strengthen the affected muscles, bones, cartilage, and tendons, therefore making the person stronger and better able to support themself. This occurs in the Repair/Rebuild Stages.

Ectoderm (outer layer)

This area is affected by issues of a connective nature, perhaps concerning territory (mostly in males), social issues in females, fear of being attacked, separation issues, and feelings of being paralyzed. The types of diseases we see in the cortex affect the mucosa (the slimy lining of specific organs of the body such as the nasal mucosa, stomach mucosa, and bronchial mucosa). The ducts of certain organs are also affected, such as the breast milk ducts, the beta and islet cells of the pancreas, the motor movements (nerves), specific areas of the eyes, the epidermis (outer layer of the skin), nails, hair, the hearing side of the ear, and the coronary arteries and veins, which are all in the cortex. In essence, every issue that relates to our 'connection', or lack of it, with the outside world shows up in the ectoderm/cortex. The biological reason for the diseases in the cortex is, basically, for the person to feel less sensitive to the issue that is affecting them, thereby allowing them to deal with it more effectively. This always occurs in the Stress Stage.

What can be read in a CT scan?

So if we can speculate that specific embryonic layers of the brain are connected to corresponding embryonic layering of an organ in a structured and organized way, if we were to look at a specific diseased layer of an organ then, in theory, we should find either activity or scarring in the corresponding area of the brain. Let's look at a series of case studies (you can view the CT scans, which demonstrate how a disease can be seen in the relative area of the brain, by visiting www.whyamisick.com):

Nephrotic syndrome

A student of mine suffered from nephrotic syndrome. From a traditional medical point of view, nephrotic syndrome is when the kidneys are damaged, causing large edemas (excessive water and protein – albumin) in specific areas of the body. In my student's case, it affected his whole body, showing up mainly in his lower abdomen and testicles. It also caused the rest of his body to swell; his face would blow up and look moon-like. In order to treat the disease, a steroid called Prednisolone is given in large doses, and the moon-face is believed to be a side effect of the treatment. However, observations of sufferers of kidney collecting tubule syndromes, suggest that the moon-face occurs before the steroids are taken and not because of them.

The issue that causes this excessive swelling is a UDIN, which involves feeling isolated and abandoned. The steroids actually cause more water to collect around the specific areas by putting the whole body into the Stress Stage. The use of diuretics can stop any further build-up, but like steroids, they are not a cure. My student's CT scan showed numerous white circles in the kidney collecting tubules area. The white circles were scarring due to calcium deposits – indicating that the disease had completed its process – and corresponded to the brain stem area (the endoderm – inner layer).

My student confirmed the reactions that occurred regarding his disease, and the UDIN that triggered the disease happened when he was two years old and became separated from his parents while vacationing in Edinburgh. He remembered how he had a strong fear of being isolated as a child, particularly if friends behaved indifferently or in an unfriendly way toward him. More important, he remembered feeling extremely anxious and stressed when his parents went out, fearing that they wouldn't return. He told me that he used to cry and scream as they left, making it almost impossible for them to have a normal social life. These emotional triggers caused the whole disease process to recur (see also page 121). After age 18 his symptoms disappeared and he is completely free of this disease now.

Anxiety

We met Lucille in Chapter 4 (see page 74); she had ongoing anxiety problems. In her CT scan it was evident that the thyroglossal ducts and the pharyngeal gland were both active at the same time. This combination of two organs being affected in this way causes acute anxiety.

In her CT scan, the rings were in the cortex area of the brain, and showed the issue in UDIN reversal and therefore in the Repair or Rebuild Stage. There were also many white spots in the center, meaning the issue was chronic, therefore repeating itself, and was continually there in the background. Hence, Lucille would go through bouts of anxiety from time to time.

Thickening of the pericardium

This client thought he had problems with his energy levels because whenever he exercised he felt out of breath and was coughing. He had been to the medical doctor who, after many tests, was unable to determine what was wrong with him. On inspection, his brain CT scan showed a clear circle corresponding to the heart pericardium. This would have caused a thickening of the skin layer around the heart. Fortunately, the client didn't have emotional heart problems (his relationship with his wife was very good), but he did, however, complain that his whole life had recently been turned upside down when an incompetent manager had threatened his job, which he loved. Therefore, the ring showed as an attack against his heart, the attack being against the job he loved.

Bone cancer

Another client, a woman with two young boys, had a bone cancer in her middle thoracic spine area. Her CT scan was taken just days before a Spike, and she experienced excruciating pain, which she reported as feeling as if someone was stabbing her in the back, along with an epileptic seizure that lasted three minutes and an ongoing migraine headache, which slowly disappeared.

Such a disease is due to a lack of self-worth conflict hitting at a very deep personal level (similar to my herniated disc described on page 32, but much deeper) along with kidney collecting tubule syndrome. This client had been forced by her business partner to do something in her company that she felt was morally wrong and on the verge of being illegal. She resolved the issue (UDIN Reversal) and then went through the Repair Stage, with symptoms of pain in the bone followed by the Spike. The pain subsided eventually. In normal medical terms this would be considered a brain tumor, but from an Advanced Clearing Energetics point of view, it is the collection of glial cells (brain reparatory cells that heal the relay) around the brain relay that collects large amounts of water during the Repair Stage. As the Spike takes place, this water is squeezed out by cramping in the brain, similar to someone trying to squeeze some juice out of an unpeeled orange.

The symptoms are severe headaches, migraines, and sometimes seizures. Sometimes the swelling of the brain presses up against the back of the eyeballs, and people see flashing lights along with the pain in a separate area of the brain. Or they experience the feeling of one eyeball being almost squeezed out of its socket. If left to take its natural course, the amount of water can subside, in which case the eyeball returns to normal. My client did experience her right eyeball being pushed out to some degree; however, this subsided very quickly.

Infertility

Another client experienced excessive bleeding and horrendous menstrual pains, and had unexplained infertility. Her brain CT scan indicated that there was a problem with her ovaries due to a UDIN – she'd had a miscarriage and this had caused her to feel a deep loss for the child, which coincided with the start of her menstruation problems. After resolving the UDIN, she conceived and gave birth to a lovely boy.

IBS

This client showed symptoms of IBS, but on closer inspection of his CT scan there were clear rings, which were broken in places with some white spots inside the rings. This meant that he was repeating the issue over and over again (see also page 121). The symptoms the client experienced were constipation and then diarrhea; however, in extreme cases, this can cause more serious diseases to develop – e.g., Crohn's disease.

Glandular breast cancer

The medical profession doesn't point out that there are two types of breast cancers and they have their origins in two separate embryological layers, but 27 percent of breast cancers are glandular cerebellum (middle brain – mesoderm), whereas 73 percent are ductal, which shows up in the cortex of the brain (outer brain – ectoderm). However, a brain CT scan of a woman in the Stress Stage of glandular breast cancer shows a very clear ring in the location of the breast cancer glands. This type of cancer is due to intense worry or an argument with a son or daughter.

The body–brain connection

Although there does need to be further research in this area to be absolutely certain that we've got this model right, there is an overwhelming amount of evidence proving that there is an amazing link between the brain and the body. This means that reading a brain CT can give a relatively accurate history of an illness, and therefore traumas that a client has experienced, as well as being able to pinpoint the ongoing issues that a client is experiencing.

In my experience of reading brain CT scans, I find that it is just as much of an art as it is a science. Interpretation of certain circles can vary from one reader to another. It does have its flaws and, as an energetic research tool, is not perfect. On the other hand, neither are modern diagnostic tools perfect. The volume of misdiagnoses has not decreased despite the number of brilliant imaging machines available now to modern medicine.

In the next chapter, we'll delve into the highly controversial area of microbes: how fungi, bacteria, and viruses are all part of the disease process and are working in symbiosis with our bodies to assist in our healing.

CHAPTER 9

BACTERIA, VIRUSES, AND FUNGI – EVIL KILLERS OR BENEVOLENT HEALERS?

'In the nineteenth century men lost their fear of God and acquired a fear of microbes.'

Anonymous

When I grew up in the 1960s, there was a 'cleaning' epidemic. Everyone was busy disinfecting everything, scared by the belief that a deadly virus or bacteria might enter their homes and destroy their lives. It was a massive fear that continues to be fueled by advertising executives and the media, who relentlessly report the consequences of not cleaning everything in your house, especially kitchen countertops and bathrooms. Complete sterility is the message.

So what did people do before the introduction of anti-bacterial products? Were we plagued by the common cold? Was diarrhea a regular complaint? Did people suffer horrendously and die terrible deaths from killer bugs and viruses, which were targeted as the criminals and villains of our modern understanding of diseases? Are vaccines and modern medical interventions *entirely* responsible for our good health?

Perhaps we're not as healthy as we're led to believe because all these issues continue to plague us, despite the introduction of new vaccines, antifungals, antibacterials, and antivirus products. Today, cleaning products are pumped into our living rooms by marketing experts who convince us of the perils of the 'nasty, evil germs' that could kill us. But at the same time, the same experts tell us about the benefits of probiotic cultures, and they're even added to foods.

We're led to believe that all bacteria and bugs are harmful, and so to put them into our body on purpose just seems wrong. Does that mean we should be adding a branded disinfectant product to our favorite yogurt as a way of cleaning 99.9 percent of all the bacteria out of our guts? Have the media and marketing companies gone mad? Or are we mad for believing what they say without really understanding the reason for microbes?

Microbes play an important part in our healing

Several years ago I attended a training course in Munich run by a medical doctor who explained how viruses, bacteria, fungi, and microbes play an important part in our healing. He described how microbes only work on specific layers of the brain. Old bacteria and fungi work on the brain stem. Newer strains work on the cerebellum. Evolutionary younger bacteria work in symbiosis with the cerebral medulla (the white matter); viruses work on the cortex.

At the time, I thought he was mad, because running through my brain was my belief system that 'fungi, viruses, and bacteria are killers.' After all, we've been taught that diarrhea is a bug you catch through poor food hygiene. Fungal infections grow in damp, warm conditions – the swimming-pool changing-room floor or our gym shoes – and can be passed on to other people. Antibiotics are the heroes, as they kill bacterial infections that threaten our health, don't they?

Ever the skeptic, I started to explore this subject, and discovered that many of the things that this doctor had said were true, but how? How do these viruses, bacteria, and fungi work? How do they assist us as biological helpers? Could they really be doing something important for us? Should we rethink the whole of Louis Pasteur's groundbreaking discovery, when he came up with our modern 'germ' theory of disease? Should we dismiss Edward Jenner's discovery that having a minor disease such as cowpox could protect a person from something as life-threatening as smallpox?

I mention these things because in the Advanced Clearing Energetics teachings, microbes are there for a positive reason; they play an important part in our healing. However, research has shown that not all strains of microbes are going to work well in every person. Some microbes will do the job they are designed to do – repair the damage after the Stress Stage – while others seem to have the effect of poisoning, maiming, or disabling a person, such as the microbes of botulism, polio, and meningitis.

ACHILLES TENDON – MICROBES IN ACTION

Adam, a friend and an NLP trainer, came to see me.
He was complaining of a small sore on his left leg

just above his ankle that wouldn't heal. It was due, he believed, to an operation on his Achilles tendon, which he'd ruptured for the second time in one year, the first time while he was playing squash and the second time when swimming.

I asked him various questions about the problem and knew there were two issues. One had to do with the breaking of the tendon, and the other with the healing of the skin on the open wound. It transpired, however, that upon returning from traveling around the world for a year, he felt depressed, as if life was over. He felt unable to relate to his friends and family since they hadn't shared his experiences.

This type of issue affects the Achilles tendon by causing necrosis in the Stress Stage, and the Repair and Rebuild Stages follow; the issue works in the same way in the wild. An animal goes through a shock of 'Life is over' and the tendon becomes weaker and weaker until it eventually snaps, then an animal can't run away from impending danger and becomes food for any predator. Therefore, in a horrible irony, the biological programming is completed.

We dealt with the 'life is over' issue and cleared out the emotions surrounding that decision, and immediately I saw his mood lift. This was great, but the real problem was the hole in his leg and the risk of infection, which several courses of antibiotics hadn't manage to treat.

Looking at the wound, it was obvious that the upper layer of skin was trying to heal but an area of about 3–4mm was still exposed and you could see pink flesh underneath it. This area is the dermis, the thick leathery *skin that protects us from being punctured. The shock that causes this layer to react is one of feeling deformed or attacked. I looked at Adam and asked him if he had felt a deformed feeling toward that part of his body since the operation. He then recounted how he remembered waking up from the anesthetic after the second operation and looking at this bandaged foot, which was suspended in mid-air, thinking 'That is not my ankle!' His voice was full of disgust and horror at what he was saying. We cleared out the shock and the decision and left it at that.*

A month later he called and excitedly told me that the wound was healing and that new skin was forming around the old hole. Two months later he called again to tell me that it had completely healed over and to thank me.

Here are some interesting facts about you as a human, discovered by the chemist Udo Pollmer. As an adult, you have 50 trillion human cells in your body, and you also have 500 trillion other cells that are bacteria, fungi, and parasites, basically not human.[1] About 85 percent of them are in your gut; there are hundreds of different strains of bacteria inside you. The question is, why? What are they doing there? It is now thought that these bacteria break down our food so we can digest it more effectively. As I mentioned previously, the newest fad in food marketing is probiotics. Undoubtedly gut health plays an important part in our lives, as this interesting quote from *The Second Brain* by Dr. Michael D. Gershon explains:

'Neurogastroenterology began when the first investigators determined that there really is a second brain in the bowel. The seminal discovery that established its existence was the demonstration that the gut contains nerve cells that can "go it alone": that is, they can operate the organ without instructions from the brain or spinal cord.'[2]

This is why in Advanced Clearing Energetics I've included the gut in the clearing of trapped energy because I recognize that microbes are biological helpers, which assist in the rebuilding of specific layers of our organs once the body has gone into the Repair Stage. So they are not active in the system until we go into UDIN Reversal.

Each one of the microbes is present in an orderly fashion. The fungi and old types of bacteria, in evolutionary terms, work alongside the brain stem (the brain stem organs are mostly to do with digestion). Candida, fungi, and tuberculosis (TB) bacteria decompose any excessive growth. Therefore, it may not come as a surprise to know that IBS sufferers often have a large amount of candida in their guts, while people with tumors in their bowels start to pass blood as the tumor is eaten away by the old gut bacteria.

Next are the cerebellum bacteria (the protective leathery skin organs). Again, TB is found here, and so are fungi – for example, in athlete's foot. Breast gland tumors also contain the TB bacteria.

In the cerebral medulla organs (the muscles, bones, tendons, cartilage), the main bacteria are staphylococcus, which rebuild the bones by filling in the gaps after osteoporosis. They do this by reconstructing the callus (by granulating callus forming tissue). Similar bacteria are also present in testicles and ovaries when they are being rebuilt.

Viruses are present in the cortex (the mucous membranes and surface areas of our body). The viruses work by reconstructing the tissue after necrosis and ulceration, and are often accompanied by a fever and/or inflammation.

How do these microbes work? It is thought that the brain tells the body to start producing the microbes as soon as the Stress Stage has started. This means that these microbes should be visible in the blood system almost immediately. Interestingly, using dark field microscopy they can be seen, but they are not active. It is also thought that the blood cells themselves produce the bacteria; again this phenomenon can be seen under dark field microscopy. (Dark field microscopy blood analysis is controversial, and banned in the USA, but uses a specific type of microscope to analyze live blood and, as the story below illustrates, can be useful in understanding microbes in action. See pictures on www.whyamisick.com.)

Another noticeable piece of information is that during the Stress Stage the body is acidic. In the Repair and Rebuild Stages the body is alkaline. In addition, there seem to be about 400 cold diseases (Stress Stage) and a further 400 warm diseases (Repair and Rebuild Stages). In the cold diseases there are fungi, bacteria, and viruses present, but no fever, and they appear to be inactive. However, the warm diseases all have active fungi, bacteria, or viral infections.

INFECTION, ANTIBIOTICS, AND HOMEOPATHY

I had my blood analyzed with dark field microscopy when I was in Australia in 2009. Everything was in good order, but the practitioner noted some activity that pointed to some bacterial infection that might occur.

What was fascinating was that this infection didn't surface in Australia, but appeared as I got on the plane to fly to the USA from New Zealand. I was very stressed while in Australia, having worked every day for over seven days without a break, followed by a day off in New Zealand. On the day of the flight to Los Angeles, I noticed that my foot was very itchy, and when I got on the plane it was quite swollen. See pictures on www.whyamisick.com

When I got to LA, I consulted a doctor at the ER and was told I had a serious infection in my right foot, which was spreading up my leg. He made a mark on my leg and told me to keep an eye on it (if you want to see the images, visit www.whyamisick.com). He prescribed antibiotics and said it could be Lyme disease (an infection caught by being bitten by a tick, named after a town in Wisconsin, USA, where it was first noticed). The doctor's diagnosis didn't surprise me because I remembered being bitten while walking through some woodland in the UK, just before leaving for Australia. However, I'd also being quite stressed by the prospect of the trip because I was unsure as to whether I could train with this material in Australia successfully, and if the expensive trip would be worthwhile. As it was, the trip was a success and I totally relaxed by the time I arrived in New Zealand. Hence, the Stress Stage followed by the Repair Stage.

Alongside the antibiotics, I took a course of probiotics to support my intestinal gut flora. As soon as the infection disappeared and the swelling went down, I stopped the antibiotics but carried on with the probiotics.

However, several years later my leg swelled up again in the same place. This time I hadn't been bitten and, instead of antibiotics, I used homeopathy and B. Propolis, a natural antibiotic made from bee pollen. In fewer than three days, the swelling and infection completely disappeared. My belief now is that prescription antibiotics merely push the issue deeper, thereby not allowing the body to complete its natural healing cycle. This is a common postulation in homeopathy.

In telling this story about my leg, I hope to show you that bacteria are being made in our blood *before* any infection appears, and the importance of working with the microbes and not against them. The overuse of antibiotics in the last 30 years has proven this factor, too. It has now become such a problem that medical doctors are being told not to prescribe antibiotics in the same way they did years ago. This is because bacteria are becoming resistant to antibiotics and are changing. An example of this is the antibiotic-resistant MRSA bacteria, which used only to be found in hospitals, but a newer form of which is now showing up in the community.

Bacteria in our system

The fact is that we live in symbiosis with trillions of bacteria and other microbes, and 85 percent of the bacteria live in our intestines, which is about 2–4lbs (1–2kg) of gut flora. If we have an issue that affects our gut, the old-style bacteria do the clean-up job by eliminating the excess cells that have been created in the Stress Stage. The viruses and some bacteria that are present in our system rebuild the cells that have been used after the Stress Stage. (See also pages 89 and 169 for the six stages and embryonic layering.)

If the body doesn't have fungi, bacteria, or viruses to do this clean-up job, then it will use the microbes that are available in the local environment to complete this healing, as the story below demonstrates.

GUT INFECTION – INABILITY TO DIGEST

When my wife and I were in Egypt with a group of friends, halfway through the week we all came down with the same stomach bug at the same time. A few days before this we'd visited a restaurant where we were significantly overcharged, which left us feeling angry and disappointed, which might be considered a minor UDIN. Two days later we had a fabulous meal in a different restaurant, the UDIN Reversal. The next day all of us came down with the same bug, the Spike.

As an experiment, some of our friends took a short course of antibiotics, I took one set of the antibiotics, and my wife took none. My wife suffered marginally more pain than the rest us, but we all got better at the same time.

My conclusion is that the body uses the bacteria from the surroundings to complete the Repair and Rebuild Stages. Taking the antibiotics helped to a degree to alleviate the symptoms, but the whole problem would, and did, disappear if it had been left alone.

If the same thing had happened in our native countries (and we were upset at being overcharged), then the body would have used the local bacteria; and it would have probably resulted in a loose bowel movement, without too many ill effects. However, in our case, we were unaccustomed to the environment in Egypt, and the body used a strain of bacteria that was literally 'foreign' to us, and caused excessive diarrhea.

What the body is doing is building up a reserve of bacteria in the blood in the Stress Stage, and then during the Repair and Rebuild Stages the microbes become active, doing their work. There are situations where the bacteria are not present in our system, and if this happens then the body encapsulates the issue. This only happens in the brain stem and cerebellum issues. We literally see fine tissue around the excessive growth. In cerebral medulla- or cortex-related issues, it doesn't repair and rebuild the used tissue that has necrotized; therefore, it leaves the body scarred and weaker.

LUNG TUMOR – CHILDHOOD FEARS OF DEATH

I worked with a person in St. Lucia who was diagnosed with a large tumor in his left lung during a routine CT scan. I questioned him at length, and he'd had no recent fear of death issues. However, when he was 18 he did fear for his life; he explained that his mother was an alcoholic and had tried to kill him.

Since he was living in paradise (his words when referring to St. Lucia), very happily married, with no issues whatsoever, lots of money, and a wonderful life, I explained that the tumor was the result of the shock when he was 18 and was likely to be encapsulated and benign (inactive). As a result, my client refused to have surgery or a biopsy, as I explained to him that any procedure would puncture the thin membrane of the tumor and might start the cells multiplying again.

When I spoke to him recently, he told me that he is thankful for his decision, and instead has had regular CT scans and is watchful of symptoms, but three years later the tumor remains unchanged.

He did ask me what would happen if he got the TB bacteria, which would eat away at this type of tumor. I explained that because the growth of the tumor had completed its process, the TB bacteria would not remove the tumor. Bacteria can be more deadly than snake venom or strychnine, but most are actually beneficial. Ironically, many are used in the production of antibiotics, as well as enzymes for detergents, for leaching out metals from low-grade ores, in the making of foods, to make certain vitamins, such as vitamin C (though these bacteria have been genetically modified), and for the conversion of milk sugar (lactose) into lactic acid. Vinegar is produced through bacterial action. Bacteria are even used in the manufacture of cocoa and coffee.

People have at least 10,000 times more bacteria inside them than there are people on Earth. Each adult human has 1,500 different microbes, of which only about 100 are potentially dangerous. In 1980, the International Committee on Systematic Bacteriology agreed to reduce the accepted number of named species of bacteria from more than 30,000 to about 2,500 species. Yet, without these organisms, life would cease to exist.

Microbes and the brain layers

Each brain layer has evolved over millions of years, beginning with the brain stem, then the cerebellum, the cerebral medulla, and ending with the cortex. As our brains and embryonic layers have evolved, so has the symbiosis with each layer. It's worth noting that while most bacteria work happily in symbiosis with our bodies, some produce waste products that cause toxins in the system, e.g., some strains of listeria. Plus, if bacteria are starved of oxygen, they produce toxins that are harmful in the Repair and Rebuild Stages.

Below I've listed each brain area and added the common microbes that do their work in the Repair and Rebuild Stages. You'll see there is an overlap between the layers: e.g., in the brain stem and cerebellum, likewise between the cerebellum and the cerebral medulla, and the cerebral medulla and the cortex.

Brain Stem

The oldest microbes are directed by the brain stem. Considered to be the 'destruction crew,' they decompose issues formed in the Stress Stage (e.g., colon, lung, kidney, or liver); this healing process takes place only in the Repair and Rebuild Stages and is usually accompanied by fever and night sweats. If no mycobacterium is available during this time, then the tumor is encapsulated in scar tissue and stays without further cell augmentation (in cancer this is diagnosed as a benign tumor). Mycobacteria start multiplying from the point of the UDIN moment to the UDIN Reversal, at the same rate as the excessive cell growth. During the Repair Stage, the bacteria decompose the excessive cell growth, and this waste is removed via the sweat glands, urine, feces, etc. Symptoms are a warm sweat, and a bad odor from the pores and breath. There could also be bleeding or abscesses forming – as the bacteria eats away at the conflict mass.[3] Common examples of fungi and bacteria used in the brain-stem-directed organs include:

- Mycobacterium tuberculosis – affects the lungs and is in the guts
- Avium-intracellulare – affects the pulmonary veins and lungs
- Mycobacterium scrofulaceum – affects the cervix
- Histoplasmosis – affects the lungs
- Cryptococcus – yeast infections
- Sarcoidosis – similar to TB
- Syphilis spirochetes – affects the genitals
- Candida – found mostly in the gut
- Listeria monocytogenes – meningitis in newborns
- Streptococcus – affects the pharynx of the throat (e.g., strep throat)

Cerebellum

Cerebellum-directed bacteria are considered the 'clean-up workers,' as they help decompose issues, such as acne or tumors, melanoma or breast gland tumors, and assist in clearing the remnants. These bacteria play a major role in helping to restore tissue by forming abscesses and filling them with scar tissue. Common examples of fungi and bacteria used in the cerebellum-directed organs include:

- Anthropophile (athlete's foot) – the most common species are microspore, epidermophyton, and trichophyton; and account for 90 percent of all fungal skin infections, commonly referred to as ringworm

- Tuberculosis – often found in peritoneum, pericardial, and pleura issues and glandular breast cancer

- Listeria monocytogenes – meningitis especially in newborns, septicemia, and encephalitis

- Endotoxins – these include bacillus, listeria, staphylococcus, streptococcus, enterococcus, and clostridium, which causes diseases with bacilli-shaped bacterium including TB, whooping cough, tetanus, typhoid fever, diphtheria, salmonellosis, shigellosis, legionnaires' disease, and botulism

Cerebral Medulla

Evolutionarily these bacteria are the second youngest microbes. Cerebral-medulla-directed bacteria (e.g., staphylococcus) take part in the process of filling the gaps in bones caused by a meltdown of callus cells, and play a major role in reconstructing the bones with granulating callus-forming tissue. Bacteria will also present in the rebuilding of cell loss (necrosis) of ovarian and testicular tissue. The bacteria that work with the cerebral medulla are more evolved; they form chains or group together to perform their repair job. Common examples of bacteria used in the cerebral-medulla-directed organs are:

- ⦿ Staphylococcus aureus (the most common), and also methicillin-resistant staphylococcus aureus (MRSA) – affects the blood

- ⦿ Tetanus – causes lockjaw

- ⦿ Cocci – diseases include pneumonia, tonsillitis, bacterial heart disease, meningitis, septicemia (blood poisoning), and various skin diseases. Cocci are round/spherical cells; they may be true spheres, e.g., staphylococci, helmet-shaped, e.g., pneumococci, or kidney-shaped, e.g., Neisseria. Cocci may occur alone, in pairs, or in groups. In pairs they are called diplococcic, threes are a triad, etc. Other group types include: fours called tetracoccus, chains called streptococcus, cubes of eight called sarcina, and irregular clusters called staphylococcus – cause pneumonia, tonsillitis, bacterial heart disease, meningitis, septicemia (blood poisoning), and various skin diseases.

Cerebral Cortex

From an evolutionary point of view, viruses are the youngest microbes. Found in organs of the ectoderm such as skin-epidermis, bronchi, the nose, intra-hepatic bile ducts, and the cervix, they are directed by the cerebral cortex. Viruses are part of the 'reconstruction' of the Repair Stage; they help replenish the tissue lost during the preceding ulceration process. Viruses start dividing and multiplying only after the UDIN Reversal. The Repair Stage involving viruses can be intense and is often accompanied by fever or inflammation. Common example of viruses used in the cortex-directed organs are:

- Human papillomavirus (HPV) – often found in the cervix and penis head
- Pneumonia – lungs
- Hepatitis – liver and gall bladder
- Herpes – genitals, lips, and the outer layer of the skin
- Flu – bronchi and larynx
- Epstein Barr – chronic fatigue
- Helicobacter pylori – stomach and epithelia cells

These viruses are also present in diseases such as cervical cancer, multiple sclerosis, chronic fatigue, the common cold, gastric flu, cold sores, smallpox, and measles.

Epidemics: Why do they occur?

Often when I'm teaching Advanced Clearing Energetics, the following question arises: why are so many people affected at once with the same infection? In this situation, the collective consciousness is affected and when, as a whole, this group resolves the issue (UDIN Reversal), then they all get the disease.

For example, before, during, and after World Wars I and II, there was a massive increase in tuberculosis (TB). What is noticeable, however, is that the increase in the number of people suffering from TB occurred slowly from World War I to II, and by then there were many hospitals dedicated to its treatment. These hospitals have now all but closed worldwide. So was this due to immunization, or has it occurred because of a shifting in mass consciousness?

TB has been in our systems for a long time. Traces have even been found in Egyptian mummies. It has been known to be a terminal illness for centuries, but since the mid-1800s sanatoriums were used to treat TB. Hermann Brehmer built the first sanatorium in Germany in Gorbersdorf, where treatment consisted of good nutrition and continual exposure to fresh air. Patients were found to recover from what was thought, at the time, to be a terminal disease.

The strange thing about TB is that the bacteria (mycobacterium tuberculosis) which cause it are known to be in the system of many people. Just because a person may have the bacteria, it doesn't necessarily mean that they feel sick, and from an Advanced Clearing Energetics point of view, it is only when the bacteria becomes active in the Repair and Rebuild Stage that is it called the disease 'TB.'

TB in Advanced Clearing Energetics terms repairs and rebuilds the lung alveoli. The relay for these cells is present in the brain stem. The conflict shock is fear of death. Obviously with two world wars and the ongoing threat of death, we would see this type of threat as very real. Many soldiers were diagnosed with TB in these wars, and often entire barracks in prisoner-of-war camps were dedicated to the treatment of this disease; it was probably due to the fact that the stress they had been going through and the fear of death abated when they were captured, and then they went into the Repair and Rebuild Stages.

The BCG (Bacille Calmette and Guérin) vaccination named after the two scientists who discovered it in France in the late 1920s is still the only vaccine used against TB. However, this is not the whole story, so before I elaborate on the use of this vaccination in our society, I want to mention that TB is very difficult to get out of the system once it is there. It is not a rare bacterium either – one-third of the population of the world has it.[4]

In order to eliminate TB from a person, an intensive drug regime of six to nine months has to be administered. It is well known that many people with latent TB hardly ever develop the disease nowadays.[5] Chemotherapy was considered as a treatment after the massive increase in TB after World War II, but the widespread use of the BCG vaccination appeared to eradicate the disease. Consequently, vaccination is heralded as the reason for the demise of TB, but this is far from the real story.

The purpose of TB

As I have mentioned, TB is due to the shock of possible invasion or a threat against a person's life (fear of death). If this is ongoing, then the person is under of lot of repetitive stress. The disease works in this way. During the Stress Stage, there is an extra increase in alveoli (these are the tiny air sacs in the lungs that allow oxygen into our blood and carbon dioxide out). This allows the person to be able to get more oxygen into the system. A person with more oxygen is better equipped to be able to get oxygen to the muscles and therefore fight more effectively; hence, overcoming the fear of death.

During this build-up of extra cells, we also see an increase in the mycobacterium tuberculosis, which lies inactive in the blood. Once the threat of the fear of death has gone, the excessive lung cells that had originally built up are no longer required, and therefore the body wants to get rid of them. The brain/body tells the bacteria to eat away at the now unnecessary alveoli cells. The symptoms associated with this removal are deep wheezing due to restricted airflow, fever, and lack of energy, and most important, coughing up blood and sputum from the depths of the lungs.

This coughing-up of blood is actually the excessive alveoli having been digested by the mycobacterium tuberculosis being expelled. The easiest way to get these unnecessary cells out of the system is to cough them up. The body uses the most obvious and easiest way to eliminate the unwanted cells: through the mouth. The problem is that it is very scary, and when people see blood in their phlegm, they think they are dying (mass media explaining the symptomology and death rate also causes the cycle of fear of death to repeat itself).

World War II was a great example of this. Once the threat had disappeared, the influx of people suffering from TB increased. Once the fear of death had dissipated along with the subsequent introduction of a vaccine and a cure, the belief systems in people changed and the disease also dissipated.

However, vaccination was not the reason for the decline in the number of deaths from TB, because this was happening before the introduction of mass immunization. According to the Commonwealth Year Book No. 40, the official figures on TB deaths were as follows:

- 1921: 3,687,000
- 1931: 3,167,000
- 1941: 2,734,000
- 1951: 1,538,000
- 1961: 447,000

So although mass immunization using BCG only started after World War II in 1945–1948, the decline was already happening before then.

Changes in diet and hygiene standards as a result of understanding how active bacteria get into the system really reduced the death rate. This, together with the cause disappearing – a fear of death during the world wars – indicates that the reduction in TB is unlikely to have been due to mass vaccination.

To prove this point, there has recently been an increase in TB cases in the USA, which has been attributed to people coming from infected areas and breathing the airborne bacteria over others. But this doesn't make sense, since people have been traveling into the USA from infected areas for the last 50 years or more. From an Advanced Clearing Energetics point of view, however, a more likely reason is that the increase is due to the aftermath of 9/11, as many people in the USA are now living in a continual state of fear. A third of the world's population has the TB bacterium in them already, so the increase is as likely to be from the fear created by the actions of Al-Qaida, fueled by a power-hungry US military machine and the media.

I live in Canada, near Toronto, and the difference in political attitudes between these two neighbors is quite staggering. People don't carry guns in Canada, and therefore their attitude to the threat of an attack is very different. Their military power is minute in comparison to that of the USA. Al-Qaida did not attack Canada. Canada didn't send troops to the Second Gulf War.

Statistics from both countries regarding TB show that there was a difference after the 9/11 attacks in the USA. Both countries have consistently seen a reduction in TB. In

Canada it continued to decline after 9/11 but there was a blip in the USA, as mentioned in an article on TB published by the Office of Enterprise Communication Media Relations Center for Disease Control.[7]

> 'In the United States, the latest national surveillance data show a significant, but slowing, decline in the case rate of TB.'

I also discovered that in 2004 the Center for Disease Control reported the lowest rate of TB ever recorded (with records going back as far as 1953). It went on to say that the 3.3% decline from 2003–2004 was the smallest in less than a decade, compared to an average annual decline of 6.8%.

This fits with the Advanced Clearing Energetics theory that the decline stopping in the years 2003–2004 would have been after the height of the stress during 2002 following the 9/11 attacks in 2001 and the invasion of Iraq in 2002–3; remember that TB is the Repair and Rebuild Stages of the fear of death conflict; therefore, there would be a delay, and the US reported total eradication of TB before these events.

What is also interesting is that Canada had no increase in TB incidence during this time. A report on TB in Canada up to 2006 shows no change in the rate of decline in the years 2001–6 in all provinces.[8]

Disease in smaller social groups

On a smaller scale, regarding epidemics, I worked with the staff of a school for severely learning-challenged teenagers in the UK. One day in 2005, the principal told me he'd been suspended after being accused of stealing funds from the school. After a month of intense investigation, he was found innocent, but during this time the suspended principal and all his students, who really liked and respected him, endured the stress of the investigation.

When he was exonerated, he went back to the school, and carried on with his job, and the students were very happy about his return. What was interesting, however, was that two weeks later most of the students and staff and the principal came down with a stomach bug. The catering department was blamed for the outbreak, but from an Advanced Clearing Energetics perspective, this was the Spike of some information that could not be digested. What is surprising is those staff members that had instigated the whole investigation did not get the stomach bug. He told me that they were the ones who had to work day and night to get the school back to normality. There is natural justice, so my friend told me.

This is not an isolated incident, and I've also seen pockets of people in training sessions get the common cold, bar a few individuals. The question is, why do the majority get the issue while a small minority remain healthy? Surely this virus should attack everyone. The only explanation seems to be in a mass belief system that affects a group with similar belief systems (think what happens when large groups of people get together for a sports game or a concert – there is a field that affects everyone en masse). I'm sure you have experienced this type of field if you have ever been involved with a group of people and, unwittingly, you find yourself dragged into something that you would never normally do: e.g., dancing, or taking on a challenge at work as a group.

This is a recognized phenomenon and described as

'morphic fields'[9] by Rupert Sheldrake, a biochemist and author, in his groundbreaking book *A Sense of Being Stared At*. What Sheldrake explains is that we are not mechanistic machines, but living organisms that have fields around us much like that of a magnet. These fields have a kind of inbuilt memory and can explain such things as paranormal behavior, which is not as uncommon as we are led to believe. These fields also allow birds to fly in perfect formation, guide mass migration of herd animals, and also allow us to know when people are thinking about us, even when they are on the other side of the world. He believes that 'the mind itself, and what the mind can do is almost virgin territory.'[10] If you're interested in learning more, Rupert Sheldrake has written a number of fascinating books on the subject, and Lynne McTaggart's brilliant book *The Field* also covers it in great detail.

It is therefore not difficult to see how a whole country, a large group, or even a small cluster of people (such as a family) could become infected with a microbe simultaneously. The key is to understand that the illness is the Repair and Rebuild Stage of the problem. There would have been a common shock at the start that would have affected the whole group, and this then feeds into the group psyche, bringing everyone into reversal of the UDIN simultaneously.

In conclusion, do microbes cause disease, or is it more complex than we're led to believe? I'm fully aware that some bacteria can cause serious issues to occur. However, what we have been sold by the media and the medical profession perhaps needs to be rethought. We do need to rethink our approach to microbes, as can be found in the treatment of bladder cancer, where immunization using the

BCG vaccine has been found to be more successful than chemotherapy.[11]

So the cleaning epidemic has had an effect on all of us. I believe that this has probably been the reason why we are so much healthier than before the introduction of cleanliness, especially with modern sanitation and underground sewers, but the belief that these microbes are the reason for disease is misconstrued. It is not as simple as we have been led to believe. We need microbes in our system to survive.

In the final chapter, we'll explore the future of medicine and some new exciting ways of assisting a person to heal.

THE FUTURE
OF MEDICINE

'The doctor of the future will give no medicine but will
interest his patients in the care of the human frame,
in diet and in the cause and prevention of disease.'

Thomas Edison, American inventor

It has been many years since the idea for this book came
about. The first edition took two years to write, and the
revised edition with its subsequent updates has taken three
years. In that time, there have been many discoveries, and
the most important has been turning this amazing wealth of
information into something that a person can understand
and believe in.

In *Why Am I Sick?* I believe that this has finally been
achieved. We have a structure and a process for disease.
It is no longer just something people suddenly acquire out
of the blue, which hits them while walking down the street.
Most people intuitively know that something happened to
them to cause their illness, but what? Louis Pasteur's 'germ

theory' is the basis for how modern medicine treats many diseases. However, the theory that germs cause disease so you need to take antibiotics and add some steroids now and again in order to get well needs to be rethought.

The medical profession was born from this way of thinking and everyone bought into it, because it worked for some diseases, and then the assumption was made that every disease would respond in the same way. You 'pop' a pill and get well. What an amazing philosophy! The pharmaceutical industry embraced this 100 percent and has grown into one of the biggest businesses in the world today. Diseases are there to be eradicated, and we have a drug that someone, somewhere, will buy. In fact it worked so well that they and the medical profession were able to persuade governments and the media to believe whatever they were told.

However, we've found that pill-popping doesn't solve every ailment. Cancerous growths, psychological disorders, skin issues, irritable bowels, and strange syndromes such as Parkinson's disease or MS are supposed to have been 'cured' by now, using the magic bullet of 'dropping' a pill. All diseases should have been eradicated, or at least that what we've been led to believe is possible. But it hasn't worked.

Instead, we have a massive medical and pharmaceutical industry that has grown so large, so complicated, and so stuck in its own red tape that it has lost its way. Instead of evolving and asking fundamental questions and using science in the way that engineering has, it has carried on thinking in the same old way, refining the same protocols and doing the same thing, hoping that no one notices that what they are doing is *not* working.

If you challenge the medical profession or the pharmaceutical industry with this, you'll get nowhere; it's a closed shop. It is very similar to communism, which theorizes 'all are equal.' For a time it worked, in some cultures, but communism didn't evolve, as people realized there was more to life than the secret police and being told how to think and behave. Eventually 'the people' tore communism down in the Soviet Bloc, and something similar is happening in China, too, as the old belief systems haven't evolved with 'the people.' If the medical profession and the pharmaceutical companies don't heed this message, they will find themselves in the same position, which, in my opinion, would be disastrous, because to change medicine we need the infrastructure, not the outdated beliefs.

Emergency medicine continues to save many lives, and many drugs such as antibiotics and steroids can be crucial in those instances. There are many things that the medical profession does brilliantly, such as reconstructive surgery, healing bones, and caring for premature babies. Medical doctors know a lot, but it's time for their information to be updated worldwide.

Disease is a process

We need to think creatively and differently in order to educate the medical profession and to change beliefs from 'disease is an error (of the body)' and 'germs cause disease' into 'most diseases are due to UDINs (or shocking and stressful events).' The body has a wonderful order to how and why it creates a disease. The mind and body are connected to each other, and the environment and spirit play a massive part in how and when we react to a disease.

Fundamentally, disease is not a thing that is in our way, like a tree blocking the road, which we should cut, burn, or remove in order to go forward.

Just like a journey from A to B, which has a start, middle, and end; and scenery along the way for us to take in, so, too, is a disease a journey with the six stages and the environment all playing their part. Therefore, we need a different approach to solve the problem of disease. We need to step up, take an overview of the whole journey, and see the entire picture. That way we can establish alternative routes, a way to balance or complement our journey.

What I'm leading to is an 'integrative' approach to dealing with disease. Advanced Clearing Energetics finally allows us to take an overview of the process of a disease. It finally gives us a road map to follow, as my friend Karin Davidson (howtotap.com) said to me one day. It also gives an elegant system to assist people in healing themselves that uses the heart, the brain, the organs, and the guts. We can clear the imprints, which caused the issue to occur, and then the body does the rest and heals itself. I will explain more about that process in my next book, *How Can I Heal?* But sometimes it needs assistance by combining the strengths of alternative, complementary, and traditional medicine, as these all have their place in the healing journey. No single therapy is right for everyone; no single intervention will assist in the healing of a disease. There are times when modern medicine works brilliantly, and other times what's needed is emotional clearing techniques such as EFT and Matrix Reimprinting, complementary medicine such as homeopathy, the brilliant NES system, alternative methods such as Reiki and nutritional changes, and my recent work that is included within Advanced Clearing Energetics.

These all add to the overall picture of how we can now help people to get to the end of their journey.

Many of these practitioners will say that their method is the only way, but when we look at a disease from above, then we can see how an integrative approach of alternative, complementary, energetic, and traditional therapies is really the answer.

What is the future of Advanced Clearing Energetics?

The brilliant NES system integrates homeopathy and acupuncture in bottle form, called 'infoceuticals' (remedies that have imprinted information in them) to help people heal. Designed by Peter Fraser and Harry Massey, this system uses a quantum-measuring device to examine our human body field. It can determine imbalances in our field, and then using the infoceuticals, it assists the body, via the heart, to reimprint the field with updated information so that we get well. What Peter and Harry have done is astonishing, and the results that people are getting from the NES system are amazing – and further proof that changing biochemistry alone does not cause healing. The remedies have no active ingredients in them, yet our biochemistry changes when they are used.

Peter and I have also developed infoceuticals that work alongside the brain layers; assisting people by bringing up the UDIN moments in minutes rather than what I used to teach, which sometimes took hours. These emotional unblockers assist the brain in opening up the underlying emotional causes of the UDIN. I have been successfully using verbal emotional clearing techniques since 1992, and in that time I have worked with thousands of people. When I use the brain infoceuticals, along with another infoceutical called Liberator, the speed and depth of the clearing is incredible and very fast.

Harry has also developed a machine that can be used by a trained practitioner called the 'NES miHealth,' which uses electrical stimulation and a unique broadcast feature to send specific messages to correct the human body field, thereby assisting people in their journey back to wellness.

The NES miHealth combines three proven powerful technologies that have come out of decades of research: NES Matching software, NES Information Imprinting, and Russian Adaptive Electro Stimulation. In essence, you can put this device anywhere on your body, connect to your computer, and see on the screen an animated picture of your body showing highlights of potential problem areas for treatment. Once you have the Human Body-Field scan, you can then either directly treat that area via Informational Electro Stimulation or further refine your area of treatment with the inbuilt specific treatment area locator and use the NES miHealth's auto-treatment mode to assess when the treatment has taken effect.

Existing research and results behind the technologies are quite staggering, and NES are doing a wealth of research into the effectiveness of the miHealth. They recently had immense success with the Hungarian Olympic team in London 2012, who finished 9th compared to 21st in 2008.

'The effect of the NES miHealth on both the athletes' mental and physical wellbeing has been really great. We used the device for rehabilitation, pain relief, rejuvenation, stress relief, and recovery. The sports psychologists and physiotherapists

*used the NES miHealth as part of their routine treatments
with the team – and we're all convinced that it increased both
performance and achievement.'*

Agota Lenart, Hungarian sports psychologist

Further NES research can be seen at www.neshealth.com
/research. In 2012, NES-Health and Advanced Clearing
Energetics carried out a study to establish the effectiveness
of treatment using the brain infoceuticals with clients. The
results were very impressive, and we found that with 60 clients
there was a significant statistical proven benefit to using the
device for finding UDINs and clearing the trapped energy,
resulting in clients' wellness returning. This device has the
power to revolutionize the way healthcare is carried out.

NES have also produced NEStrition (NES and Nutrition),
where NES information is combined with the best essential
vitamins and minerals. The outcome is supplements
whose effects are two to four times greater on entering
the body's system and assisting with healing than just
taking the supplements themselves (www.neshealth.com).
Randomized Double Blind Clinical trials are being carried
out to confirm these findings.

NES Health is truly revolutionary and is being used
the world over by qualified practitioners, including many
medical doctors. Recently when I was traveling in Australia,
I met up with Rose Hayman and Cyril Bourke, and I saw
what I think is the future of modern energetic medicine
for everyday people. What Cyril and Rose have done is
to combine all of this incredible technology and create a
place where everyday people can get treatment. They call
it the Zap House. Together we are combining Advanced
Clearing Energetics with the Zap House work to create one

integrated system. A great name, and with their friendly, open, and accessible approach I believe we will see Zap Houses in every corner of the world.

Clearing emotional conflicts with EFT, NLP, and Matrix Reimprinting

When it comes to Emotional Clearing Techniques, these are imperative in dealing with disease; if you don't clear out the conflict shock and the underlying emotion that caused it in the past, then you risk the conflict reappearing over and over again. There are plenty of techniques out there, but my personal favorites are NLP (the study of human excellence) coupled with Time-Line Therapy® (the system developed by Dr. Tad James to clear deep-seated emotional conflicts and unwanted beliefs about yourself). Most people believe that changing takes a long time and many hours of therapy. Psychologists and counselors believe this. It is not the case; a trained specialist can clear a deep-seated traumatic emotion in minutes. An emotion that people have held all their lives can totally and utterly disappear in the time it takes to make a cup of tea.

Advanced Energetic Clearing actually has a system built into it that clears the imprints that caused the UDINs to occur, using what I have gained from 20 years of research into how people heal themselves. I worked with Charles Matthew and Tracy McBurney, who both use very high vibrations of energy to clear the trapped energy. I was able to discover what these great therapy practitioners were doing, and that is the process I now teach. More about this in my next book, *How Can I Heal?*

There are other great techniques that use similar principles, such as EFT (Emotional Freedom Technique) invented by Gary Craig, referred to as acupuncture without needles. It uses tapping on the end of the meridian lines along with reframing (an NLP technique) to release energy, emotions, and beliefs that are stuck in people. My friend and colleague Karl Dawson has gone one step further; using EFT he has created a technique called Matrix Reimprinting.

Also, Karin Davidson has created Soul Reconnection, a technique that goes back into the womb and clears out underlying patterns which cause a multitude of issues. Karin and myself have recorded DVD sets that show many of these techniques being used alongside each other. Visit www.whyamisick.com for more information.

I love EFT because you can self-tap when you are experiencing a negative emotion; you don't need a practitioner to do it for you and you can tap in the moment. You may look a little silly, but it's a small price to pay for the outcome. I personally got rid of the eczema on my left hand using EFT. Although even using EFT, you still need to resolve the major underlying UDIN conflict shock, and that often requires a session with a qualified practitioner in Advanced Clearing Energetics. Following that, EFT self-tapping can solve any tracks/triggers or associations.

There are other emotional clearing techniques, and all of them do similar things to NLP and EFT. Some are derived from EFT, such as TAT and Emotrance. There is also hypnosis, which is a brilliant tool for helping clients to heal. I use hypnosis with many of my clients and teach it, too.

Every illness has a meaning

In Advanced Clearing Energetics, we have a road map that explains so much, a system that can assist any practitioner to easily find the UDIN moment and clear its energetic pattern. We understand that every disease has a meaning, and somehow that seems to make resolving the issue more tolerable, and makes us more inclined to treat our body with kindness and respect, rather than asking a doctor to 'kill it' or mask its symptoms with drugs.

Developing Advanced Clearing Energetics has been a long journey, but I've learned so much during this time and have completed the promise I made to myself while walking up that hill to school, which was to find out why debilitating diseases happen. I believe I've done that, and gone way beyond what I thought I would discover, and if my mother were still alive today, I hope that she would be proud of me, proud of my spreading the word about this incredible information.

RECOMMENDED READING LIST

Dr. Deepak Chopra, *Quantum Healing*, Bantam, 1989

Karl Dawson and Sasha Allenby, *Matrix Reimprinting Using EFT*, Hay House, 2010

Peter H. Fraser and Harry Massey with Joan Parisi Wilcox, *Decoding the Human Body-Field*, Healing Arts Press, 2008

Michael D. Gershon, *The Second Brain*, HarperCollins, 1999

Bruce Lipton, *The Biology of Belief*, Hay House, 2010

Lynne McTaggart, *What Doctors Don't Tell You*, Thorsons, 2005

Christiane Northrup, *Women's Bodies, Women's Wisdom*, Piatkus, 2009

Candace B. Pert, *Molecules of Emotions*, Pocket Books, 1999

Dr Bernie Siegel, *Love, Medicine and Miracles*, Rider, 1999

O. Carl Simonton, James L. Creighton, and Stephanie Matthews Simonton, *Getting Well Again*, Bantam Books, 1986

ENDNOTES

Foreword – Karl Dawson and Sasha Allenby

1   EFT (emotional freedom technique) is a self-help tool, based on the Chinese meridian system (the same system used in acupuncture), which involves tapping on meridian end points in the body while tuning into and verbalizing a specific health or emotional issue. This helps to clear disruption from the body's energy system and restore health and emotional balance.

Chapter 1: The Beginning of Advanced Clearing Energetics

1   World Health Organization, Fact Sheet No. 297, 'Cancer'; http://www.who.int/mediacentre/factsheets/fs297/en/; accessed January 2013

2   Null, G., Dean, C., Feldman, M., Rasio, D., Smith, D. 'Death By Medicine,' Oct 2003; http://www.webdc.com/pdfs/deathbymedicine.pdf

3   Segerstrom, S. and Miller, G. 'Psychological Stress and the Human Immune System: A Meta-Analytic Study of 30 Years of Inquiry,' *Psychological Bulletin*, July 2004; 130(4); 601–30

4   Patterson, N. 'The Ghost in Your Genes,' (Horizon BBC Science, November 3, 2005; season 42, episode 9);

http://www.bbc.co.uk/sn/tvradio/programmes/horizon/
ghostgenes.shtml

5   Reik, W. and Surani, A. *Genomic Imprinting: Frontiers in
    Molecular Biology* (IRL Press, 1997)

6   Lipton, B., Bensch, K. *et al.* 'Microvessel Endothelial
    Cell Trans-differentiation: Phenotypic Characterization,'
    Differentiation, 1991; 46: 117–33

7   Visiongain, 'Leading Anti-Cancer Drugs: World Market
    Prospects', *2011–2021*, February 2011; http://www.visiongain.
    com/Report/578/Leading-Anti-Cancer-Drugs-World-Market-
    Prospects-2011-2021

8   Loewenberg, S. 'The Cost of Hope: Doctors Weigh the
    Benefits of New Drugs Against Sky-high Costs,' *Molecular
    Oncology*, 2010; 4(3): 302; http://www.elsevierscitech.
    com/pdfs/molonc0910/thecostofhope.pdf

Chapter 2: Are Diseases, Pain, or Cancer a Mistake; or Do They Occur for a Reason?

1   Campeau, P., Foulkes, W., Tischkowitz, M. 'Hereditary Breast
    Cancer: New Genetic Developments, New Therapeutic
    Avenues,' *Human Genetics* 2008; 124(1): 31–42

2   Walton, G. 'Some Long-held Links Between Genes and
    Diseases Called into Question, June 2011; http://www.
    thedoctorwillseeyounow.com/content/public_health/
    art3322.html

3   Lipton, B. *The Biology of Belief* (Mountain of Love, First
    Edition, 2005)

4   Lipton, B., Bensch, K. *et al.* 'Microvessel Endothelial
    Cell Trans-differentiation: Phenotypic Characterization,'
    Differentiation, 1991; 46: 117–33

5 Darwin, F. in letter to Moritz Wagner, October 13, 1876; http://www.fullbooks.com/The-Life-and-Letters-of-Charles-Darwinx29407.html

6 Briggs, D. 'Environmental Pollution and the Global Burden of Disease,' *British Medical Bulletin*, 2003; 68:1–24

7 Dolk, H. and Vrijheid, M. 'The Impact of Environmental Pollution on Congenital Anomalies,' *British Medical Bulletin*, 2003; 68: 25–45

8 Joffe, M. 'Infertility and Environmental Pollutants,' *British Medical Bulletin*, 2003; 68: 47–70

9 Boffetta, P. and Nyberg, F. 'Contribution of Environmental Factors to Cancer Risk,' *British Medical Bulletin*, 2003; 68: 71–94

10 Anoop, J. *et al.* 'Air Pollution and Infection in Respiratory Illness,' *British Medical Bulletin*, 2003; 68: 95–112

11 Rushton, L. and Elliott. P. 'Evaluating Evidence on Environmental Health Risks,' *British Medical Bulletin*, 2003; 68: 113–28

12 English, J. *et al.* 'Environmental Effects and Skin Disease,' *British Medical Bulletin*, 2003; 68: 129–42

13 Katsouyann, K. 'Ambient Air Pollution and Health,' *British Medical Bulletin*, 2003; 68: 143–56

14 Ahlbom, A. and Feychting, M. 'Electromagnetic Radiation: Environmental Pollution and Health, *British Medical Bulletin*, 2003; 68: 157–65

15 Järup, L. 'Hazards of Heavy Metal Contamination,' *British Medical Bulletin*, 2003; 68: 167–82

16 Rushton, L. 'Health Hazards and Waste Management,' *British Medical Bulletin*, 2003; 68: 183–97

17 Fawell, J. and Nieuwenhuijsen, M. 'Contaminants in Drinking Water: Environmental Pollution and Health,' *British Medical Bulletin*, 2003; 68: 199–208

18 Zhang, J. and Smith, K. 'Indoor Air Pollution: A Global Health Concern,' *British Medical Bulletin*, 2003; 68: 209–25

19 Cullinan, P. and Newman Taylor, A. 'Asthma: Environmental and Occupational Factors,' *British Medical Bulletin*, 2003; 68: 227–42

20 Stansfeld, S. and Matheson, M. 'Noise Pollution: Non-auditory Effects on Health,' *British Medical Bulletin*, 2003; 243–57

21 Little, M. 'Risks Associated with Ionizing Radiation: Environmental Pollution and Health,' *British Medical Bulletin*, 2003; 68: 259–75

22 Willett, W. 'Balancing Lifestyle and Genomics Research for Disease Prevention,' 2002: 296;(5568): 695–698 DOI: 10.1126/science.1071055 (Willett, 2002)

23 Nijhout, N. 'Metaphors and the Role of Genes in Development,' Department of Zoology, Duke University, Durham, North Carolina 27706, 1990; 12(9): 441–6; http://www.ncbi.nlm.nih.gov/pubmed/1979486

24 http://www.aicr.org.uk/GrantsstartingJune2012.stm'; accessed March 11, 2013

25 Gdanski, R. 'Cancer is not a defective Gene'; http://www.alive.com/articles/view/19726/cancer_is_not_defective_genes

26 Ibid.

27 Lipton, B. *The Biology of Belief* (Mountain of Love, First Edition 2005)

28 Siegal, B. *Love, Medicine and Miracles* (HarperCollins, 1986)

29 Siegal, B. 'Waging a War Against Cancer Versus Healing Your Life'; http://berniesiegelmd.com/resources/articles/waging-a-war-against-cancer-versus-healing-your-life/

30 'Placebo: Mind Over Medicine? Medical Mysteries,' Silver Spring, MD, Discovery Health Channel, 2003

31 Greenberg, G. 'Is it Prozac or Placebo' *Mother Jones,* 2003: 76–81

32 Moseley, J. O'Malley, K. *et al.* 'A Controlled Trial of Arthroscopic Surgery for Osteoarthritis of the Knee,' *New England Journal of Medicine,* 2002; 347(2): 81–8

33 Ray, C. in interview with virologist Dr. Stephan Lanka, October 27, 2007; http://www.psitalent.de/Englisch/Virus.htm

34 University of South Carolina Chernobyl Research Initiative; http://cricket.biol.sc.edu/Chernobyl.htm

Chapter 3: What Causes a Disease?

1 Null, G., Dean, C., Feldman, M., Rasio, D., Smith, D. 'Death By Medicine,' Oct 2003; http://www.webdc.com/pdfs/deathbymedicine.pdf

2 Brignell, J. 'The Complete List of Things that give you Cancer (According to Epidemiologists); www.numberwatch.co.uk/cancer list.htm

3 Segerstrom, S. and Miller, G. 'Psychological Stress and the Human Immune System: A Meta-Analytic Study of 30 Years of Inquiry,' *Psychological Bulletin,* 2004; 130(4); 601–30

4 Kopp, M. and Réthelyi, J. 'Where Psychology Meets Physiology: Chronic Stress and Premature Mortality – the Central-Eastern European Health Paradox,' *Brain Research Bulletin,* 2004; 62: 351-367

5   McEwen, B. and Seeman, T. 'Protective and Damaging
    Effects of Mediators of Stress: Elaborating and Testing the
    Concepts of Allostasis and Allostatic Load,' *Annals of the
    New York Academy of Sciences*, 1999; 896: 30–47

6   McEwen, B. and Lasley, E. *The End of Stress As we Know It*
    (Washington National Academic Press, 2002)

7   Lipton, B., Bensch, K. *et al.* 'Microvessel Endothelial
    Cell Trans-differentiation: Phenotypic Characterization,'
    Differentiation, 1991; 46: 117–33

8   McCrathy, R. and Atkinson, M. 'The Electricity of Touch:
    Detection and Measurement of Cardiac Energy Exchange
    Between People,' Institute of HeartMath, 1998; http://www.
    heartmath.org/research/research-publications/electricity-of-
    touch.html

9   Barton Furness, J. *The Enteric Nervous System* (John Wiley
    and Sons, 2008)

Chapter 4: Disease Affects Everything

1   Lipton, B. *The Biology of Belief* (Mountain of Love, First
    Edition 2005)

2   Pert, C. *Molecules of Emotions* (Scribner, 1997)

Chapter 5: The Six Stages of Disease

1   Weinstein, J. 'Role of Helminths in Regulating Mucosal
    Inflammation,' Springer Seminars in Immunopathology,
    2008: http://www.vitals.com/doctors/Dr_Joel_Weinstock/
    credentials#ixzz2Oc5U4Hu6

2   Fergusona, D. and Warner, R. 'Have We Underestimated the
    Impact of Pre-slaughter Stress on Meat Quality in Ruminants?'
    Meat Science, 2008; http://www.meat-food.com/allfile/
    techpaper/2008/Have we underestimated the impact of pre-
    slaughter stress on meat quality.pdf; accessed March 11, 2013

3   Lipton, B., Bensch, K. *et al.* 'Microvessel Endothelial Cell Trans-differentiation: Phenotypic Characterization,' *Differentiation*, 1991; 46: 117–33

4   Ibid.

5   Ventegodt, S., Andersen, N. J., and Merrick, J. 'Rationality and Irrationality in Ryke Geerd Hamer's System for Holistic Treatment of Metastatic Cancer,' *The Scientific World*, 2005; 5, 93–102 ISSN 1537-744X; DOI 10.1100/tsw.2005.16

6   Wake Forest University Baptist Medical Center. 'Stress May Help Cancer Cells Resist Treatment,' *ScienceDaily*, 2007; http://www.sciencedaily.com/releases/2007/04/070410103023.htm; accessed March 26, 2013

Chapter 6: Why Diseases Keep Recurring

1   van der Kolk, B. 'Posttraumatic Therapy in the Age of Neuroscience,' *Psychoanalytic Dialogues*, 2002; 12(3): 381–92

2   Guochuan, E., Condie, D. *et al.* 'Functional Magnetic Resonance Imaging of Personality Switches in Women with Dissociative Identity Disorder,' *Harvard Review of Psychiatry*, 1999; 7(2): 119–22

3   Watson, J. and Crick, F. 'Molecular Structure of Nucleic Acid (DNA),' *Nature*, 1953; 171(4356); 737–8; http://www.nature.com/nature/dna50/watsoncrick.pdf

4   Patterson, N. 'The Ghost in Your Genes,' (Horizon BBC Science, November 3, 2005; season 42, episode 9); http://www.bbc.co.uk/sn/tvradio/programmes/horizon/ghostgenes.shtml

Chapter 7: The Spike

1   Thuo, J. 'A New Hypothesis on Spontaneous Remission of Cancer, 2005; www.second-opinions.co.uk/thuo-hypothesis.html#.UT5ZINF35XA; accessed March 26, 2013

2   'The Healing Crisis. AKA: The Cleansing Reaction, the
    Detox Reaction and the Herxheimer Reaction'; http://www.
    falconblanco.com/health/crisis.htm

3   Kunz, R., Tetzlaff, R. *et al.* 'Brain Electrical Activity In Epilepsy:
    Characterization Of The Spatio-temporal Dynamics
    With Cellular Neural Networks Based On A Correlation
    Dimension Analysis,' 2000; http://citeseerx.ist.psu.edu/
    viewdoc/summary?doi=10.1.1.28.1285

4   Spiroux de Vendômois, J., Rouillir, F. *et al.* 'A Comparison
    of the Effects of Three GM Corn Varieties on Mammalian
    Health,' *International Journal of Biological Sciences,* 2009;
    http://www.ncbi.nlm.nih.gov/pmc/articles/PMC2793308/

Chapter 8: Our Brain – the Biological Relay Switch and Recorder of Every Disease

1   Smith, M., Saisan, J. *et al.* 'Depression Symptoms and
    Warning Signs, 2013; http://www.helpguide.org/mental/
    depression_signs_types_diagnosis_treatment.htm;
    accessed March 12, 2013

2   Servick, K. 'A Leap Forward in Brain-controlled Computer
    Cursors,' Stanford University School of Engineering, 2012;
    http://engineering.stanford.edu/research-profile/leap-
    forward-brain-controlled-computer-cursors; accessed March
    26, 2013

3   Fraser, P., Massey, H. and Parisi Wilcox, J. *Decoding the
    Human Body Field* (Healing Arts Press, 2008)

4   'Chemotherapy Drugs Side Effects,' Stanford Medicine
    Cancer Institute; http://cancer.stanford.edu/information/
    cancerTreatment/methods/chemotherapy.html; accessed
    March 26, 2013

5   Duke University. 'Emotional Memories Function In Self-
     Reinforcing Loop,' *ScienceDaily*, 2005; http://www.
     sciencedaily.com/releases/2005/03/050323130625.htm;
     accessed March 26, 2013

6   Jankowsi, K. 'PTSD and Physical Health,' 2007; http://www.
     ptsd.va.gov/professional/pages/ptsd-physical-health.asp http://
     ptsd.about.com; accessed March 26, 2013

7   Kaiser, E. and Gillette, C. 'A Controlled Pilot-Outcome Study
     of Sensory Integration (SI) in the Treatment of Complex
     Adaptation to Traumatic Stress,' *Aggression, Maltreatment
     & Trauma*, 2010; 19: 699–720; http://www.traumacenter.org/
     products/pdf_files/SI Txt for Adult Complex PTSD article-
     Spinazzola.pdf; accessed March 9, 2013

8   Grafton, S. 'Contributions of Functional Imaging to
     Understanding Parkinsonian Symptoms,' *Current Opinion in
     Neurobiology*, 2004; 14(6); 715–9

9   Tanji, J. and Mushiake, H. 'Comparisons of Neural Activity in
     the Supplemental Motor Area and Primary Motor Cortex,'
     Cognitive Brain Research, 1996; 3(2); 143–50; http://wexler.
     free.fr/library/files/tanji (1996) comparison of neuronal
     activity in the supplementary motor area and primary motor
     cortex.pdf

Chapter 9: Bacteria, Viruses, and Fungi – Evil Killers or Benevolent Healers?

1   Humphries, C. 'The Deep Symbiosis Between Bacteria
     and their Human Hosts is Forcing Scientists to ask: Are
     We Organisms or Living Eco Systems?' *Seed*, 2009; http://
     seedmagazine.com/content/article/the_body_politic/P2/;
     accessed March 26, 2013

2   Gershon, M. *The Second Brain* (Harper Perennial, 1999)

3   Guinée, R. *Les Maladies Mémoires de l'Evolution* (Amyris, 2005)

4   World Health Organization. 'Tuberculosis. Fact Sheet No. 104,' 2013; http://www.who.int/mediacentre/factsheets/fs104/en/

5   Center for Disease Control and Prevention. 'Treatment for TB Disease,' 2013; http://www.cdc.gov/tb/topic/basics/default.htm; accessed March 26, 2013

6   http://www.theoneclickgroup.co.uk/documents/vaccines/Immunization Graphs PPT - RO 2009.pdf

7   Office of Enterprise Communication Media Relations CDC; 'Fact Sheet: Tuberculosis in the United States,' 2004; www.cdc.gov/media/pressrel/fs050317.htm; accessed March 17, 2005

8   Ellis, E. ' Tuberculosis in Canada Community Prevention and Control Public Health Agency Canada – Ottawa'; www.phac-aspc.gc.ca

9   Sheldrake, R. *A Sense of Being Stared At* (Crown and Three Rivers Press, 2003)

10   Goodnow, C. '"Sixth Sense" May Be Biological,' *Seattle Post-Intelligencer, 2003;* http://www.sheldrake.org/Articles&Papers/articles/staring_interview_SeattlePI.html

11   Urdanta, G., Eduardo, S. *et al.* 'Intravesical Chemotherapy and BCG for the Treatment of Bladder Cancer: Evidence and Opinion,' *European Urology Supplements*, 2008; 542–7; http://eu-acme.org/europeanurology/upload_articles/Urdanate PDF.pdf

INDEX

ABOUT THE AUTHOR

Richard Flook is the president of the International Association of Advanced Clearing Energetics. Since early childhood, after the divorce of his parents and subsequent death of his mother from metastasized breast cancer, he has felt a deep compulsion to find an answer as to why this disease struck down the most important person in his life. At the age of 30 he realized his dream, and through the intensive study of NLP while successfully running the family business, he eventually became a master and qualified trainer of NLP; and worked for major blue chip organizations including J.P. Morgan, Chase Manhattan Bank, Samsung, and Sony Ericsson.

Richard went on to develop Advanced Clearing Energetics, introducing his groundbreaking material worldwide and becoming a pioneer of accelerated and advanced learning techniques. He achieves incredible results with terminally ill clients, and also works with everyday people, assisting them in transforming their lives at the deepest level. Richard is renowned for teaching complex skills with ease, so that new practitioners and potential trainers can achieve the same miraculous results that he does.

Richard is a native of the UK and now lives near Toronto, Canada, with his lovely wife, Kristin; and their son, Oliver.

www.whyamisick.com

Printed in the United States
by Baker & Taylor Publisher Services